Beyond
Blue Suits and Resumes

Proven Methods
Insure Your Job-Finding Success

Annette L. Segall

York Publishing Co.
Shaker Heights, Ohio 44120

Beyond Blue Suits and Resumes

This publication is designed to provide accurate and authoritative information with regard to the subject matter covered. It is sold with the understanding that the publisher is not engaged in rendering legal or other professional advice.

York Publishing Company
16781 Chagrin Blvd. #336
Shaker Heights, Ohio 44120

Designed by Lachina Publishing Services

Library of Congress Catalogue Card Number 94-062174
Cataloging in Publication

Segall, Annette L.

   Beyond blue suits and resumes: proven methods insure
your job-finding success/Annette L. Segall
   p.   cm.
   Includes index.
   ISBN 0-9634940-3-1

   1. Job hunting. 2. Employment interviewing.
3. Resumes. I. Title.

HF5382.7.S44   1995
650.14

Printed in the United States of America

10 9 8 7 6 5 4 3 2 1

To anyone who needs a job now or in the future.

CONTENTS

❖

ACKNOWLEDGMENTS

❖

This book could not have been written without the help of many people. I am especially indebted to Jerry Hill, Vice President of Training, Management Recruiters International; Louis R. Scott, Vice President for Corporate Development (Ret.), Management Recruiters; and the late Jack Gubkin. These wonderful people were the outstanding instructors for the Sale to Success program upon which this book is based.

Professors Donald M. Wolfe, Donald K. Freedheim, and Dianne Tice provided expertise in psychology and social psychology. Jeannemarie Caris-McManus and Robert E. Maher contributed their business planning perspectives.

Lori, Jeffrey, and Paul Segall and Joan Berman Segall made invaluable suggestions, and my husband and best friend, Ben Segall, provided the encouragement and support that made the book possible. Many people offered helpful suggestions, including Rachal Rapoport, Barbara Smoloff, Carol E. Rivchun, Helga Sandberg Crile, Richard Gildenmeister, Diana Tittle, Belleruth Naparstek, Hal Becker, Carolyn Dickson, Larry Barbushak, Robin B. Lake, Eleanor Shankland, Sara E. Stashower, Susan R. Hurwitz, Ginger Kuper, and Marvin Jacobs. Among the many resourceful librarians whose expertise is so valuable to job seekers, I am particularly indebted to Kathy Savage and Susan V. McKimm. Finally, a vital contribution was made by the hundreds of job seekers whose real-life stories help illumine the book.

CHAPTER 1

Can You Insure Your Job-Finding Success?

IS THERE ANYTHING LIKE *EMPLOYMENT* INSURANCE?

We buy insurance of all kinds to protect us against events like fire, theft, and collisions because their consequences can be so severe.

What about unemployment? For most people, being out of work certainly isn't rare. In fact, we can count on it. According to the U.S. Department of Labor, the average 18-to-30-year-old American has worked for 7 1/2 different employers and will have to find at least 10 jobs during his or her career.[1]

But who ever heard of taking out *employment* insurance? (States do, of course, provide limited *un*employment compensation, but it doesn't cover first-time job seekers, people who quit their jobs, those who have exhausted their benefits, etc.) Employment insurance may not have been necessary years ago when getting an education, finding a job, and doing it well usually provided employment security. But things have changed.[2]

The New Realities

In the new corporate world order, *having* a job isn't enough. *Doing a very good job isn't either.* Even superstars, like Lee Iacocca, get fired. If you're working, you should, of course, continue to do everything possible to meet the needs of your employer. Upgrade your skills. Use every legitimate means to become indispensable.

But some things are beyond your control. Like the gigantic economic quake that is shaking the foundations of the business world, covering our landscape with dislocated workers. Corporate pyramids, stacked with layers and layers of managers, seemed secure—until the ground under them broke open. Now it's clear that they, like the great monuments of ancient

Egypt, represent an old culture. Replacing them are new organizational forms, like "spider webs," "shamrocks," and "starbursts."

In a shamrock organization, for example, a core staff is assisted by a larger number of people who provide services on a contract or temporary basis. Former Harvard Business School Professor Charles Handy estimates that less than half of the work force in the industrialized world will be in "proper" full-time jobs by the beginning of the 21st century. The rest will be self-employed, part-time, and temporary employees.[3] The future is fast approaching. The *New York Times* reported recently that "there are 24.4 million part-time and temporary workers, representing 22% of employed Americans."[4]

Your Employment Security

Whether you're working or not, highly educated and skilled or not, *ultimately your employment security—and your independence—come from being able to take control and find another job. Quickly.* Knowing how to do that is your employment insurance. That's what this book provides.

The best time to invest in it is when you're working, *before* the quake hits. Fortunately, it's never too late, because employment insurance is different from other kinds of insurance. You don't have to get it in advance. Buying flood insurance after the deluge won't do much good. But you can benefit from *employment insurance* at any time in your career.

HOW CAN YOU SURVIVE THE ECONOMIC QUAKE?

Reframe: Take a Good Look at Your Situation

You cannot control the quake, but you can decide how you'll perceive and prepare for it. And that goes a long way to defining it and determining its outcome for you.

When the economy is reinventing itself and businesses are re-engineering, why not reframe yourself, your job search, and the job market? According to Charles Handy, reframing is "the ability to see things, problems, situations or people in other ways . . . [to] think of them as opportunities, not problems . . . Companies, at their best, do this all the time."[5]

Even the most cataclysmic acts of God present opportunities. To begin again. To rebuild. When the familiar has vanished, you're forced to look at what's left. The old economic security has gone. So has corporate fidelity and paternalism.

But loyalty to yourself is alive and well. So is your sense of belonging to your trade or profession. By reframing, you can look at your situation from a perspective which could open up a host of possibilities. You can position yourself for the tremendous changes and opportunities that are emerging. Whole new industries and thousands of businesses are being created in our extraordinarily dynamic economy. Innovative software alone, reaching the market daily, changes the way we do business and paves the way for entirely new enterprises. Opportunities are out there. If you're prepared to look for them, you'll find them.

Your job search is a voyage of discovery—a chance to explore some of these possibilities. If you're proactive, you'll be in a better frame of mind to do that. Why not choose an active, "take charge" role, like an:

- ◆ explorer/treasure hunter/miner
- ◆ private eye
- ◆ investigative reporter
- ◆ researcher/scientist
- ◆ entrepreneur

Can you picture yourself in a diver's gear? Sherlock Holmes' cap? Or a reporter's trench coat? Delving into gold coins from a sunken Spanish galleon or crucial evidence to unravel the mystery. Interviewing the CEOs of mid-sized firms for your article about virtual manufacturing.

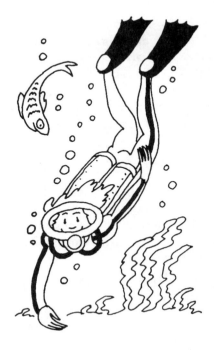

Are you a researcher, sifting through the results of your survey? Or a businessperson, exploring ways to provide better services to your customers? All of these activities require keen observation and excellent analytical skills.

You are proactive, constantly pursuing information and opportunities—skills you'll use to solve the case of the unemployed person!

Inc. Yourself:[6] *Be Entrepreneurial*

Have you ever thought about being self-employed? At a recent workshop, 70 job seekers were asked: What do the words *entrepreneur* and *entrepreneurial* mean to you? Their responses were almost invariably positive:

"Being your own boss . . . Independent . . . Self-starter . . . Creative . . . Happy . . . Successful . . . Decisive . . . Risk-taker . . . In control." Not surprisingly, many of these job seekers, like hundreds of others who have been asked recently, overwhelmingly indicated that their employment goal—either immediate or long-term—was self-employment. The American dream.

What does this dream have to do with finding employment NOW? Does it mean you have to start a business? Buy a franchise? Not at all. You can use the entrepreneurial approach in many ways, as you'll see in Chapter 4. Thinking of yourself as self-employed offers lots of advantages. Most important is the sense that you're in control, no longer at the mercy of external forces. That in itself will make you feel better about yourself.

When you stop to think about it, you've always worked for yourself— not for the XYZ Widget Company or whoever signed your paycheck. In the past, what you thought about your relationship to your employer may not have been so critical. Now it is, because it's apparent that your company won't take care of you no matter how many years you've worked there. Regardless of the details of your agreement with your employer and how benevolent they may be, you are basically a contract worker. You have a job as long as you meet their needs. That's the cold reality. So you are, in a very real sense, self-employed. And self-insured.

Plan to Survive

Isn't it harder to succeed in business than to find a job? Not really. Basically, they're the same. Successful businesspeople will tell you that when they launched their business, they may not have had an elaborate business plan, complete with a carefully worded mission statement. But somehow, they knew:

- ◆ What they were selling
- ◆ Who needs it
- ◆ How they would reach these people (clients, customers)

When you answer these same basic questions, you'll have a marketing plan that will help guide you to your next job. That's quite different from the hit-or-miss approach most job seekers use. A seat-of-the-pants search may not have been so bad years ago when the job you found might have lasted 30 to 35 years. But jobs like that are as extinct as the brontosaurus. Now, the average job lasts only 4.5 years and you're going to be job hunting again. If you're going to be doing something *that* important *that* often, it makes sense to do it well. Use methods that work.

But getting that help hasn't been easy. There's no central mechanism to provide solid information and assistance to job seekers. What we have is a non-system, a patchwork of government departments, some not-for-profit agencies, and a plethora of businesses—resume services, employment agencies, etc. You deserve more than that.

BEYOND BLUE SUITS AND RESUMES OFFERS EMPLOYMENT "INSURANCE"

Do You Need It?

Maybe you don't. You're job hunting—but you've had lots of interviews. And several terrific job offers! In fact, your only problem is deciding which job offer to accept. Right?

If that's your situation, congratulations! You can fast-forward to the last chapter, Negotiating Your Compensation.

But if you're like most job seekers, you're struggling. Who would have thought it would be *this* hard? Or take *this* long? After all, you've got a lot going for you. Education. And skills. You've got a nice blue interviewing suit. Your resume looks good. *But it's not getting you through the door.* How can you do that? And once you get an interview, *how do you convince them to hire you?*

Proven Methods

This book contains no magic pills, but it can help insure that you'll find employment because it:

1. is *based on RESULTS*
2. *focuses on your needs, offers specific suggestions and lots of examples*
3. offers a "take charge" approach that can make your job search a productive, positive experience
4. provides a *flow chart, an innovative visual guide*, to your next job

1. Based on results. Thousands of people have benefited from the approach and techniques which are the core of this book. More than 1,100 graduated from a program called Sale to Success. Eighty-three percent of these graduates found employment within 90 days of completing the program. Others have benefited from workshops and counseling using the same concepts and techniques.

Many of these people were victims of corporate restructuring. They had worked hard, played by the rules, and assumed that as long as they performed well and stayed out of trouble, they would always have a job.

Then the "rules" changed. Suddenly, what they thought happened only to others happened to them. Overnight, their way of life, plans, income, security, and even identities were shattered. But with some help, they picked up the pieces and moved ahead. You can too.

2. Focuses on YOUR needs in the '90s. *Beyond Blue Suits and Resumes* takes you step by step through the process that helped these people find employment quickly. They're people like you, from office and shop workers to engineers and bankers, from entry-level to top management. The results of research on 351 other job seekers is also included.[7]

3. Offers a "take charge" approach. You may not want to be a "take charge" person, but do you have a choice? The best way to deal with the new realities is to change what you can change. Decide what you want, prepare, and go for it. The alternative is to make a big lap and wait for your job to fall into it. Can you wait that long?

4. Provides a flow chart. You probably didn't need a road map to get a job years ago. In fact, employers may have sought you out because of your solid experience and skills. You never really had to search for a job. Until now. Now you know that there's more to finding a job than a good resume and a nice blue suit.

THE JOB-FINDING FLOW CHART HELPS YOU

Gain Perspective

If finding a job seems like madness, the flow chart on page 7 shows that there's method in it. The process is, in fact, quite logical. The flow chart provides an overview, showing the major elements of the job-finding process and how they relate to each other. That in itself helps you gain some control and perspective. Here you are, at the left side of the map. Jobs—many more than can be depicted—are out there on the right. In fact, you're surrounded by a world of opportunities.

Job Finding Flow Chart

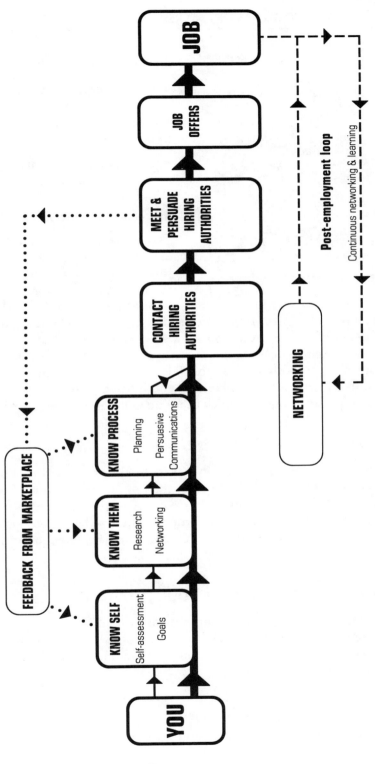

See What's Essential

The flow chart pares down the whole process, making it clear that getting hired requires only two things. These are basic, but not simple. You must:

◆ meet with a hiring authority[8] (a decision maker who has the authority to hire you).

◆ persuade that person to offer you a job.

If a job is all you want—any job—you can probably find one at your local mall. Just apply where you see the Help Wanted signs.

But that's probably not the kind of job you're looking for. If you are reading this book, you're more likely to be pursuing a career. And you want an opportunity to satisfy your interests, to use your education, experience, and talents to get a good job. You're much more likely to accomplish that if you go through the steps—assess yourself, set your goal, plan how you'll reach it, and implement your plan. Give these pivotal activities the time and energy they deserve.

Understand the Numbers Game

In order to persuade decision makers to hire you, you've got to meet them, usually after contacting them by mail or phone. Picture a kind of funnel, starting with a larger number of contacts. From these, you'll set up meetings with hiring authorities, some of which will generate job offers. Finding a job is a numbers game. *Not* meeting with enough hiring authorities is the *biggest roadblock for job seekers. Could it be yours?*

THREE MAJOR PHASES OF YOUR JOB SEARCH

What separates you from these decision makers—and your next job—is inadequate information. Gaining that knowledge is the learning experience of your life, taking you on a fascinating voyage of discovery where you'll find out about:

◆ yourself

◆ them—the jobs, companies, industries, and hiring authorities

◆ the process—planning and persuasive communications

1. Know Yourself. Initially, you're in a transition. Whether you're searching for your first job or "between engagements," you owe it to yourself to take a good look at yourself, where you've been, where you want to be, and what you have to do to get there.

2. Know Them. Researching who will buy your services is a great chance to explore! Who's doing what? What do they need? Who are the decision makers?

3. Know the Process: Planning and Persuasive Communications. Although planning and persuasive communications seem to be limited to one phase of the job-finding process, these activities are so basic that they permeate the entire book. Persuasive communications, for example, starts in with self-assessment in Chapter 2, because you must know something very well in order to sell it effectively. The explanation of persuasive communications continues with goal setting, planning, preparation, asking the right person, listening, presenting a good case which emphasizes benefits, overcoming objections, and closing. Finally, all these skills come together when you negotiate your compensation (Chapter 17), because negotiations are a specialized form of persuasive communications.

The three phases of your job search—know yourself, know them, and know the process—correlate with the three questions in your marketing plan: What are you selling? Who needs it? How will you reach them?

JOB-SEARCH JUGGLING AND FEEDBACK LOOPS

Job-Search Juggling

The essential movement of the flow chart is in a single direction, from YOU at one end to your next JOB at the other. But finding employment is really more of a juggling act. You're pursuing several different activities at once—researching companies at the library, networking to learn more about decision makers, planning how to reach them, following up on leads, preparing for meetings with hiring authorities, writing thank-you notes, and following up. The more balls you keep in the air, the more options you'll have.

Feedback from the Marketplace

In addition to doing all these things simultaneously, you'll be incorporating what you learn, as the Feedback from the Marketplace loop indicates.

What is the marketplace telling you? Do you have what they need? If your head's red from beating against a brick wall, should you reassess your goals or reevaluate your plans?

Listening to the marketplace is a critical part of the process. Even wonderfully trained and skilled people, like physicists and aerospace engineers, can find themselves dead-ended by changes in the marketplace. By adapting to the needs of the marketplace, however, they can find new ways to use their many talents. That's something every businessperson must do. As you go through the process of exploring for needs and listening carefully to what potential employers are saying, you'll develop something very valuable—excellent antennae.

Post-Employment Loop

You will find a job. But don't get *too* comfortable when you do. There's no way to insure that you'll stay with that company for the rest of your days—unless it's your company. The word from corporate veterans on the "front lines" is: "Keep up your networks. Network actively. Stay connected with people outside your organization."

An outplaced executive added the Post-Employment Loop to the flow chart. It's not suggesting that you begin looking for another job the minute you find one. But it reminds you to keep alert to what's going on outside, as well as within, your organization.

YOU WILL FIND EMPLOYMENT!

Take Charge

You're self-employed and recognize that the best way to find a job is to be positive, curious, and enterprising, a combination explorer/investigative reporter/Sherlock Holmes. Wearing those hats will make your job search much more interesting and open up many more options for you.

Use Methods That Work

Nothing works for everyone *all* the time. But some methods work *most* of the time. The techniques described here have proven effective for thousands of people like you.

Most job seekers hear the standard advice: You've got to "sell yourself." But no one explains what that means. Or how you go about doing it. Even worse, it sounds pushy and conceited—not the sort of person you are or want to become.

That's an unfortunate stereotype. Selling is an honorable profession which is at the heart of the entire economy. When you think about it, you realize that nothing happens until somebody sells something to someone. Quality salespeople don't manipulate and deceive. They tell the truth attractively.[9]

Beyond Blue Suits and Resumes explains how you do that. The process is persuasive communications, which involves assessment, setting goals and planning, research, asking questions, listening carefully, presenting a good case based on the other person's needs, overcoming objections, and asking for a decision.

Now that you've "Inc.'d" yourself and need to think and function like a businessperson, you're selling your services. You have a great deal to offer your employer and this book explains how to do that professionally.

Be Systematic

You can dramatically shorten the time it takes to find a job by following our suggestions conscientiously and systematically. By working at it full-time (40 hours a week), you should be able to find employment within three months. If you have a clearly defined and attainable goal, it will take much less time. You may not find the job of your dreams immediately. But it will be employment (and not merely the "flipping hamburger" variety).

Be Flexible

Some of the recommendations in this book may ask you to stretch farther than you're accustomed to. Can you learn to be more proactive and positive about yourself? Tragically, many very competent, well-educated people waste months, even years of their lives, experiencing untold anguish, loss of income and self-esteem, because they don't fully understand the job-finding process or lack one or two acquirable skills.

What is each month of unemployment costing you?

- ◆ If you could shorten your unemployment by one month, what would you gain financially?
- ◆ How much is it worth psychologically to be employed?
- ◆ How much is it worth to know that you can cope effectively with unemployment not only now but in the future?

Compare those oppressive costs with the "cost" of following our suggestions and learning the skills of persuasive communications. More than ever, these are *survival skills*. They will not only help you find employment, they'll help you stay employed, improve your career prospects, and enhance your interpersonal communications.

Learning and using these skills is a solid investment in your financial and emotional well-being. It's a policy that will pay you rich dividends. If you want a job within three months, follow these suggestions systematically and enthusiastically. They'll work—if you do!

CHAPTER 2

❖

Self-Assessment:
Getting to Know You

Who are you?
What do you enjoy doing?
What motivates you?
What makes you feel joy and pride in your work?
What do you want to accomplish in life?
*What would you attempt to do if you were absolutely sure you wouldn't fail? What
are you doing now? Is there a gap between the two? Why? What's holding you
back?*[1]

KNOW YOURSELF

The first phase of your job search involves asking yourself questions that many
of us never ask—or answer. You may have been too busy earning a living and
coping with day-to-day needs. Right now, you may feel that you can't afford
the luxury of "dreaming" about what you *really* want to do with your life.

But can you afford *not* to? How did you feel about your last job(s)? Did
you love it? Were you eager to get started each day? Or has your experience been that "work is something you have to be 'compensated' for
because it robs you of living? . . . The test is how you feel each day as you
anticipate that day's experience. The same test is the best predictor of
health and longevity."[2]

You began this book as an investment in employment insurance, but
you could also think of it in terms of life—and health—insurance. Since
you're the beneficiary, why don't you go for a complete check-up? Self-
assessment means examining yourself. For job seekers, there might be at
least three distinct but related objectives, including assessing yourself:

1. For yourself—exploring deeply, going back to your earliest memo-
    ries, examining the big picture to enhance your own understanding

of who you are and what you want to do in your life. (This exploration continues in the discussion about goals in Chapter 3.)

2. For your more immediate job-finding needs, to inventory your skills, interests, and accomplishments.

3. From a potential employer's perspective, to help you find a job.

These are all important objectives, but since this book is about finding employment (rather than career development), the emphasis is on #2 and #3.

KNOW YOURSELF IN TRANSITION

Are You Ready to Begin Job Hunting?

Whether you're a recent graduate looking for your first substantial job, are reentering the job market, or have just lost your job, you're in transition. Job seekers in all three categories often experience a tremendous range of feelings. Many describe a dizzying roller-coaster of emotions, conflicting feelings of hope and fear, confidence and confusion.

If you've lost your job, you may feel that you've suffered a devastating blow and are very angry or depressed. People respond differently to losses like these and have different ways of coping, some taking a much longer time to bounce back than others. Even though you may feel you've "got to find a job right away," going out on interviews immediately might not be wise.

Some experts feel that it's counterproductive to dwell on your loss. They believe that in the long run, you'll probably save time by taking a few days (two weeks maximum) to acknowledge your feelings, grieve over your loss, and then begin to do some things that will help you feel good about yourself before launching your job search. Here are some suggestions to help you move on.

En Route to a Positive Attitude:
Get Rid of Depression and Anger

Psychologists Donald K. Freedheim and Dianne Tice suggest the following techniques for dealing with depression and anger:[3]

◆ **Do something nice for yourself.** Treat yourself to a movie, a nice walk, a visit with a good friend.

◆ **Walking and other physical exercise** are therapeutic—excellent ways to shake off a bad mood.

- **Remind yourself of past successes,** personal as well as work-related accomplishments.
- **Create small successes.** Do something you have always wanted to do. If you learn a new skill, you accomplish two objectives simultaneously.
- **Volunteer to help others.** Freedheim suggests bringing something (especially meaningful is something you've made yourself) to a school, an ill person, a nursing home, or hospital. "If you don't know anyone in those circumstances," he advises, "simply ask who has not been visited lately and keep that person company. They will be delighted to see you."

"Look for opportunities to be helpful," Tice suggests. "Even little acts of kindness—holding the door for the woman with the baby carriage—will make you feel better."

- **Compare yourself with those who are less fortunate,** in a nursing home or hospital, for example. Gain perspective on your situation by recognizing that you have much to be thankful for. Helping others brings other personal rewards. You will feel competent and appreciated. Whether you are tutoring a child, helping to build a home for the homeless, or assisting a nonprofit with your marketing expertise, you will probably learn something valuable from the experience. And you may even make some good networking contacts. Don't expect something in return. But something good may happen eventually.
- **"Being with others,** especially friends, is the most common strategy which people use to feel better," Tice found in her study of strategies for changing moods.

  Many job seekers find that participating in a support group is very helpful. They are not only comforted by knowing that there are other competent people facing the same plight, but they may also gain leads and other useful information. There is, however, the danger that support groups can become *too* comfortable, a club-like refuge from the cold world outside.
- **"Avoid social brooding,** ruminating over your plight again and again with anyone who will listen," warns Tice. That's not only a turn-off for them, she explains, but her research shows it makes you angrier. Share your feelings once or twice with your spouse, a friend or a counselor, if you have not already done so.
- **"Writing about your experience may help,"** Tice suggests, "but don't overdo it. Then move on."

- **"Do something constructive."** After your "cooling off" period, you'll be in a better frame of mind to do something useful.
- **Reframe.** "Looking at the problem from another perspective can help you take control of it," Tice advises. "By changing your interpretation of what happened, you can begin to change your feelings about it."

Your Positive Attitude: A Necessity

Reframing and the other techniques described here will not only help you deal with any anger and depression you may have, they will help you develop a positive attitude. That's essential. You can study all the proven job-finding techniques and go through the motions of implementing them. But unless you communicate a positive attitude, you're starting this journey with your feet tied. One way or another, you've got to untie those knots. Your attitude is the single most important ingredient of your success in finding a job.

These suggestions are offered at the beginning of the book because you may need them now. You will probably need them later as well. Maintaining a positive attitude in the face of rejection is one of the most difficult things job seekers face. Come back to these suggestions. Use them when you're feeling "down." They can help you keep the disappointments, which are almost invariably a part of any job search, in perspective. And can help you get moving again.

Some Exercises for Probing Deeply

Anyone can benefit from self-assessment. Whether an in-depth probe is necessary right now, however, may depend on how well your interests and abilities mesh with opportunities in the marketplace. If you're exploring a career change, you'll be gathering information about yourself and analyzing it.

Social psychologist Donald M. Wolfe[4] suggests that you search for themes and patterns in your life to gain a clearer understanding of yourself. He proposes several specific exercises to help you conduct your search:

1. Play. Make a list of 20 things you enjoy doing. What do you do when you don't have to do anything? What do you *wish* you were doing? What do you fantasize about doing?

2. Life history. Think back to your earliest recollections and write your autobiography. The more detail, the better. It may be useful to organize and write your history in terms of periods of stability and change/transitions. How would you describe the phases in your life, such as childhood, adolescence, high school years, college, and employment? When you made transitions in the past, what factors influenced them?

Write about your experience when you were doing something very well and really enjoyed it. Where do you feel fully alive? When you have completed these exercises, review what you have written. What common themes do you see? Are there patterns of strength, skill, and activity which pervade these experiences? Wolfe suggests that you draw a chart of your life, pointing out the highs and lows of your experiences, to help you clarify and express your life history.

3. Get feedback from people who know you well. What strengths and talents do others honestly see in you? What weaknesses? What do they see you doing that excites you?

4. Psychological instruments, such as the Myers-Briggs Type Indicator and the Strong Interest Inventory, may suggest some new options for you. Career centers at colleges and universities, as well as private career counselors, provide these kinds of services.

The exercises will help you identify themes in your life which have implications for your career and job choices. Writing, Wolfe notes, is an important part of the self-discovery process because after you've put your thoughts, impressions, and feelings into words, you can gain some emotional distance from them.

TAKE STOCK OF YOURSELF

Your Education, Employment, and Personal Activities

Once you know your career direction and are ready to find employment, you'll want to inventory your experiences, skills, abilities, and accomplishments. In addition to your work and school experiences, include important personal activities as well.

Take some paper and create an Education Worksheet by listing the items below and filling in the blanks. These facts about you will be incorporated into your presentations to potential employers. Don't hesitate to ask family members, former classmates, and colleagues for their input. They may be able to help you recall some achievements you have overlooked.

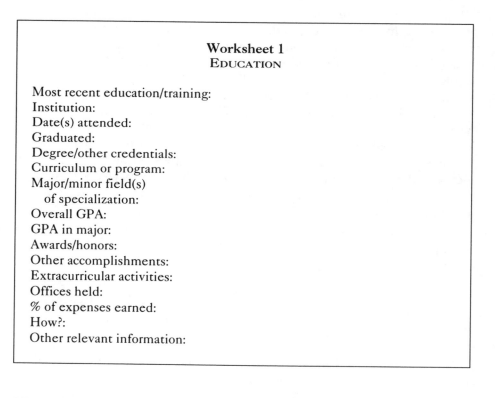

Worksheet 1
EDUCATION

Most recent education/training:
Institution:
Date(s) attended:
Graduated:
Degree/other credentials:
Curriculum or program:
Major/minor field(s)
   of specialization:
Overall GPA:
GPA in major:
Awards/honors:
Other accomplishments:
Extracurricular activities:
Offices held:
% of expenses earned:
How?:
Other relevant information:

What Have You Learned Lately?

If you're in the process of learning a new skill or improving an existing skill, include that information on your worksheets also. If you're unemployed, this could be an excellent time to fill in some education/training gaps. You'll not only benefit personally, but employers will be impressed with your commitment to learning.

Joan, the public relations manager for an international food company, hired a former homemaker in her mid-fifties with only two years of experience in public relations. The critical factor? The applicant was a *recent* college grad who had learned desktop publishing *on her own while working full time.* Joan's judgment paid off: Her new hire was an outstanding employee.

Your Employment Worksheets

Starting with your most recent job, think back over your employment history (not more than 10-15 years) and write down all the relevant facts about what you did. As much as possible, be specific and quantify relevant information, using dollar or percentage figures. If you initiated, led, developed, or created something, be sure to state that. Use a separate sheet of paper for each position, list the items on Worksheet #2, and fill in the blanks.

Worksheet 2
EMPLOYMENT

Most recent employer:
Dates of employment:
Brief description of employer:
Your title:
Your major duties and
   responsibilities:
What skills and abilities did you
   learn and use to perform these?:
Accomplishments (specific):
Special recognition:
Other relevant information:

Personal Activities

Your community activities could be the key to a new career or your next job. They are particularly important if your employment history is limited or if you are re-careering. Organizing a major community event, raising substantial amounts of money, or getting high visibility for a nonprofit agency demonstrate that you have sophisticated skills which are in demand in the workplace.

Starting with your most recent activity, outline your volunteer endeavors. Not being paid does not mean that you did not work. You did—and it's time to give yourself credit for it. Get some more paper and do a worksheet for each major community activity.

Worksheet 3
PERSONAL ACTIVITIES

Community activities

Dates:
Organization:
Major functions of the organization:
Your position:
Your function/responsibility:
Accomplishments (specific):
Skills you developed and used:

Hobbies and Interests

Skills/abilities you developed
    and used:
Accomplishments:

FOCUS ON ACCOMPLISHMENTS

What Are Your Major Accomplishments?

Be sure to allow enough space on each of your worksheets for your achievements because identifying them and writing them down is so important. As you look back over your employment history, what are you most proud of? What are your most satisfying experiences? What did you do that made a real difference to your employer and colleagues?

Many people, it seems, never stop to think about that. Regardless of their backgrounds, they're at a loss to describe their most significant contributions.

"I was taught you're not supposed to brag," or, "I was just doing my job" are the common refrains. But bragging is not what this is about. You're simply analyzing the past and describing what you did. If your major achievement involved a team effort, analyze your role and give yourself credit for that. Did you:

- ◆ prepare any original papers or reports?
- ◆ make or participate in any technical accomplishment?
- ◆ design a new product, system, program, plan?
- ◆ implement any management decision or administrative procedure?
- ◆ identify a need for a plan, program, product or service?
- ◆ take the initiative in solving a problem, recognizing an opportunity?

When you look at your work history, ask yourself what would have happened if you had *not* done something. You may not think it was such a big deal to recommend and incorporate a new software program for your claims processing department. But the costs in that department would have been almost 60% higher without that software program.

Did you receive special recognition? Awards? Letters of appreciation? Maybe there's no engraved plaque, but what about excellent evaluations? Promotion letters? *Now's the time to pull out all those things and make the most of them!* If you're still employed, get everything you might need, including statements from authoritative sources, to back up your claims.

After some probing, most job seekers can recall a time(s) when they did something noteworthy—performed "above and beyond."

Charlotte Anne's resume gave little hint of her multimillion-dollar accomplishments. When her job as assistant high school principal in a northern New York State community was eliminated in 1978, she found work as a finishing supervisor for the town's major employer.

From that modest beginning, she worked her way up to supervisor of budget and administration for one of the company's 30 divisions. Her dissatisfaction with the slow, error-ridden budgeting process prompted her to develop and help design a new budget system which became a model for the entire $3.7 billion corporation. As a result, the budgeting process, which had taken many managers three to four months each year, could now be done much more accurately and effectively in a few hours, saving the company millions of dollars each year.

Charlotte Anne's efforts were recognized by a plaque. *And* by the elimination of her job in 1993. An unassuming woman, her overly modest resume began with: "Versatile professional with successful careers in business and education." Not surprisingly, that resume wasn't opening any doors, and she experienced months of job search frustration. Happily, that ended when Charlotte Anne purchased a learning center franchise. She's now putting her considerable skills, energy, and enthusiasm to work to help people learn and develop her business.

Another example. The manager of a truck stop station for BP America noticed that there was a significant error rate in the company's statewide shipping service. Paul developed and implemented a strategy for improving customer service which not only reduced the errors but cut down on overtime expenses for union personnel.

As a result, the company saved $276,000 a year ($240,000 in shipping costs and $36,000 in overtime expenses), while significantly improving customer satisfaction. That was only one of his contributions. Altogether, Paul had saved the company at least $750,000 in addition to enhancing customer service. Before we asked him to give us more detail about his work, he had insisted that he had done "nothing special."

Still Struggling to Identify Your Accomplishments?

Ken also insisted that he was "just doing my job." He's a computer technician (they call him systems operator) for a small economic forecasting company. All 50 employees rely on their computers to do their work, and Ken's job is to keep those machines humming so no billable hours are lost. When the company moved to another location recently, he did lots of advance preparation and planning. Then, Ken worked all weekend to make sure that every computer was in place and functioning properly when the staff arrived at the new office Monday morning.

His achievement? No downtime. When he learned that the combined billable rates for the staff totaled $3,000 an hour, he realized that, by avoiding downtime for two days, he had saved the company more than his entire year's salary.

The contributions you make may not be so dramatic, but they could still be significant. Barbara is an all-purpose secretary for a small not-for-profit agency. Recently, the receptionist quit without warning. The office was in total disarray. The phones were ringing incessantly and clients were clearly impatient because of the delays. Everyone realized that the most essential person in the office was gone.

But Barbara quickly took charge. She knew from previous experience that temporary receptionists had caused a lot of confusion, misdirecting calls and paperwork. So she concentrated on recruiting and training a replacement. Within a week, a permanent receptionist was orchestrating calls at the front desk and everyone was smiling again. Not only had Barbara saved the agency money (the temporary agency charges an additional $5 per hour), but more important, she quickly restored order and professionalism.

How much is that worth? It's not easy to put a dollar value on normalcy, but the reputation of the agency and its ability to gain support (including funds) depend heavily on its professionalism. By restoring that so efficiently, Barbara had made an important contribution.

Why Are Your Accomplishments So Important?

The past is prologue. Your achievements back up your general statements with specifics and provide prospective employers with evidence. Anyone can talk about being a good manager, working well with people from diverse backgrounds, meeting deadlines, etc. Can you prove it?

Being aware of your accomplishments also contributes to your confidence and self-esteem by reminding you how valuable you have been. And still are! "I still think about what I was able to accomplish," comments Paul, the former truck stop manager, "especially when things are not going so smoothly in my business, and that helps me feel good about myself."

Don't discount the small, less easily measured accomplishments. Receptionists who are invariably polite, pleasant, and efficient may not be able to furnish figures showing that they save or make money for the company. But by keeping the office running smoothly, they improve productivity and teamwork. Salespeople who go out of their way to please customers may not make the evening news. But satisfied customers are what the business is all about. They're responsible for repeat business and the company's excellent reputation. How long would there be a business without that?

"MINING" YOUR WORKSHEETS

What else can you pull from your worksheets? When you consolidate the information in each category, what conclusions can you draw? Do you see a pattern of increasing responsibilities? What are your strengths? What new skills have you been learning?

What functions have you performed at work, school, or in the community? Have you managed? Trained? Developed? Created? Initiated? Built? Analyzed? Researched?

The key facts about you are embedded in these worksheets. They are not only the "hard," objective facts, like age, gender, and years of experience, which are quite easily verified. There are other facts about you, which may be considered "soft." They are more subjective, but if you can *substantiate them*, they can give you a big competitive edge.

How do you describe yourself? Industrious, reliable, conscientious, disciplined, persistent, an effective leader? Can you verify these claims? Do your accomplishments provide proof? How do others describe you? Ask your friends. What evidence can they give?

Here are the facts about Amy, a young college graduate with limited work experience.

Facts About Me

Facts (As I See Myself)	Accomplishments, Evidence
Good student	GPA: 3.5; Dean's list 4 semesters
Creative	Designed and contributed newsletter articles, press releases, etc.
Leadership	President, Public Relations Student Society of America
	President, Residence Hall Association

Facts (As Others See Me)	Accomplishments, Evidence
Creative	As PR intern, planned and oversaw Baby Day at major hospital
Community-minded	Active in many organizations, Cystic Fibrosis Club, campus activities
Hard-working	Worked part-time while attending college full-time, maintaining excellent GPA

Take some paper and list key facts about yourself and evidence to back it up.

FACTS ABOUT ME

Facts (As I See Myself)   Accomplishments, Evidence

Facts (As Others See Me)   Accomplishments, Evidence

Accentuate the Positive

Some ancient mariners among you may remember a song that was popular decades ago—"You've Got to Accentuate the Positive, Eliminate the Negative." Hopefully, you're doing this in general. Here's a very specific way to focus on the positive.

On another piece of paper, list things you like about yourself and things that others like about you. Don't exclude anything. Some things will be obviously relevant to the workplace. For instance, people may like you because you have a great sense of humor. That's a big plus in any situation. It can also be that they like you because you're wonderful with children. If your work is not related to children, that might not seem to be very pertinent, but list it anyway. Being wonderful with children suggests that you're patient, tolerant, flexible—characteristics that are, in fact, very desirable in the workplace.

Things I Like About Me   **Things Others Like About Me**

Your Values

One of the most important reasons for assessing yourself is determining what is important to you at this time in your life. What motivates you?

Money?
Status/prestige?
Freedom/independence?
Recognition?
Opportunity to learn?
Security?
Leisure time for family/friends?

What drives you now may be quite different from what motivated you in the past. Your own experience and needs, as well as the marketplace, may dictate changes. Shortly after she graduated from college, for example, Jodi was moved by a desire to help less fortunate women. "I found a job doing social work at a home for battered women," she said. "But I guess my idealism faded when I found myself working 80 hours a week. I felt burned out and needing a career change."

After assessing herself, Jodi realized that there were many ways she could use her communications and other skills. Encouraged to pursue a sales career, she got professional training, built up her confidence, and is now happily employed as an account executive with LCI International, a telecommunications company.

The rapidly changing marketplace continues to dictate career changes for millions of workers, including many well-educated, highly skilled people like Joe, a mechanical engineer. After more than 25 years in the railway supply industry, it looked as though Joe had reached an impasse. His company was not only downsizing—it was also relocating out of state, a move that he chose not to make. Unfortunately—or so it seemed at the time—there were no other railway supply companies within commuting distance.

"I felt I had two choices: either beat my head against the wall or look at a related field. A friend had an interesting suggestion: technical writing."

Although writing had not been a major responsibility in Joe's previous jobs, Joe recognized it as one of his skills. He contacted Penton Publishing, Inc., a business publications company, to explore opportunities.

"The only opening they had at that time was not a good fit. But three months later, an associate editor's position became available and they called me

back. The chief editor of my magazine was looking for someone with an engineering background and I was hired!"

That was 1988. Since then, Joe has been thriving as the associate editor of *Power Transmission Design.*

Knowing what you *can* do and do well—as well as what you don't like to do—are important first steps. Deciding what you *want* to do is another. Goals and goal setting are the subject of Chapter 3.

EMPLOYMENT INSURANCE CHECKLIST

✓ Are you ready to begin your job hunt now or are you too angry or depressed to begin?

✓ If you've lost your job, did you take time to grieve over your loss?

✓ Do you have a positive attitude?

✓ If not, what are you doing to help you develop a positive attitude?

✓ Did you list your interests, talents, and skills?

✓ Did you create an education worksheet listing important facts and major accomplishments?

✓ Did you create an employment worksheet for each job, listing important facts and major accomplishments?

✓ Did you create a personal activities worksheet, listing important facts and major accomplishments?

✓ What do you like about yourself?

✓ What do other people like about you?

✓ Do you know what motivates you?

CHAPTER 3

❖

Goals: Where Are You Heading?

WHY BOTHER WITH GOALS?

"When a man does not know what harbor he is making for, no wind is the right wind." [Seneca, 8 B.C.—65 A.D.]

We can all picture that hapless boat, lurching without purpose, as each gust of wind whips its sails. Like a job hunter who lacks focus, it's pushed and pulled by external forces.

What harbor are you heading for? Once you decide, you'll be energized to reach it. And you'll gain a remarkable sense of control. Goal setting is a crucial element in your employment insurance policy.

Setting a goal is one thing. Achieving it is another. This chapter explains goal setting and outlines some techniques to help you reach your goals. The rest of the book is about accomplishing what you set out to do.

HOW TO SET YOUR GOAL

Define It So It's Useful to You

The Goal Setting/Planning Guide outlined later in this chapter (page 35) begins with the statement: *The more specific you can be, the better.* It's not enough to say you want a good job . . . a position in a Fortune 500 company . . . a lot of money . . . or a marketing position. These objectives are too ambiguous. To be really useful, your goal should be:

1. *Achievable,* but not too easy. Stretching helps you make the most of your mental, as well as physical, muscles.
2. *Measurable.* If it's not measurable, how will you know when you have achieved it?

Financial security, for example, is a worthy objective, but it's not an appropriate goal because there's no way to know you have reached it. Once you define financial security as $50,000, $500,000, or $5,000,000 in savings, you will *know* when you're there.

Specificity is powerful for another reason. It helps you to see yourself enjoying the fruits of your labor. The more distinct your goal, the easier it is for you to envision achieving it. And that vision helps to propel you forward.

You may know exactly what you want to do and have what it takes to get there. If that's your situation, you can fast-forward to page 33: How to reach your goal. But chances are you picked up this book because you're not certain about where you're heading.

Developing Goals: Who Has Difficulty?

Almost everyone. In fact, it may be the hardest thing we have to do. Several of our survey respondents reported that the most troublesome aspect of being unemployed related to goals: "Finding a direction in which to go . . . difficulty focusing on something specific . . . feel a lack of direction . . . do not know what I want to do . . . hard to formulate goals with confidence."

What a contrast with the way we plan more trivial pursuits! Think how much time and attention we lavish on buying a car or choosing a vacation. Even a party can consume many hours of planning and preparation. But then we'll choose a job—or even a career—on the basis of a tidbit of information or a casual remark!

Why Goal Setting Is So Hard

Setting our sights on a career goal is more difficult, of course, because so much is at stake. And there are so many unknowns. Even after a careful self-assessment, you've probably concluded that there are lots of things you *can* do and do well. And there may be many things you'd *like* to do.

Deciding on a career goal usually involves a bit of crystal ball gazing as well. That's always chancy. Now that our economy is shifting so rapidly, it's dicier than ever to predict what training and skills will be in demand in the future. A few years ago, for example, authoritative sources warned of a severe shortage of scientists. Simultaneously, Ph.D. physicists and chemists were coping with diminishing openings, a condition that has not improved.

Making a career decision, which usually requires investing significant amounts of time and money, is a formidable challenge for anyone. For those who lack confidence and fear failure, it can be overwhelming. They tend to procrastinate, have trouble getting organized, and taking risks. We can certainly empathize, but it's important to put risk-taking in perspective.

Risk-taking is something we're aware of *when we act. But NOT acting is also risk-taking!* As one extraordinarily successful businessman put it: "Doing something costs something. Doing nothing costs something. And quite often, doing nothing costs a lot more."[1] Why not ask yourself the questions high achievers ask themselves before making decisions:

- ◆ If I fail, can I live with the consequences?
- ◆ What is the *worst* thing that can happen?
- ◆ Can I live with that?

If necessary, they start all over again, no worse off than if they had not acted in the first place. Often, they have learned something valuable from the experience, even if the outcome was not what they had hoped. So they're still better off.

How many times have you stretched way out for a fast ball in tennis or baseball? This is going to be tough, you thought. Not sure you could get it. But you went for it anyway. Isn't it amazing how many times you actually got that ball? And how great it felt when you did!

Learning What You Don't Want Helps Too!

You may not know what you want to do yet, but you may be really sure about what you *don't* want. That was Mary's situation.

> *"After 13 years as a LPN (licensed practical nurse), I knew that I wanted to get away from hands-on nursing. But that was the only thing I was sure of. I really didn't know what I wanted and I had no idea about how to find a job. So there I was, 38 years old with my new degree in English. That was 1990. It took me a year to find a job!"*

With a clearer focus, Mary probably could have saved herself a lot of frustration—and time. She pursued jobs in college recruiting and journalism but, despite relevant experience, she was repeatedly turned down. Happily, a career counselor helped Mary see how she could combine her health care experience and newly honed skills in communications. Hired as a customer service representative for a managed-care provider, she was soon promoted to health services coordinator, a position she finds challenging and satisfying.

If You're Not Focused, Others Will Focus for You

Don, an attractive young man with five years of experience in sales, was looking for a "quality company that will make a commitment to its people." He knew he didn't want to continue selling copiers. And was quite sure he didn't want to sell cellular phones either. But he didn't know what he *did* want. In almost four months of "looking," he was no further along than when he started. Since he didn't know what he wanted, other people were telling him what to do.

Why don't you get into telecommunications, some suggested. Others claimed that hospital supplies were big in this area. What about commercial real estate? The suggestions were all over the lot, leading Don in the direction of *their* interests. Not his.

When Don was asked what he'd really like to sell, he said his real interest was sports equipment or something else related to sports. The obvious next step for Don was to identify and research the relevant companies, both at the library and through knowledgeable people. If he really worked at that, he could probably get enough information within a month to set a specific goal. Then he could move ahead to reach it.

How Research Can Help You Define Your Goal

Thirty thousand! That's an old estimate of different kinds of jobs in the U.S.—and new positions and whole categories of occupations are being created almost daily. It's an incredible range of opportunities to choose from. And there are great resources to help you research them. The *Dictionary of Occupational Titles* (DOT), for example, lists more than 12,000 job titles with detailed descriptions of each title.[2] Most libraries also have the *Occupational Outlook Handbook*, a major source of vocational guidance information for hundreds of occupations. The Handbook describes what workers do on the job, details the training/education needed, and gives some idea of the availability of jobs.[3]

All libraries have some resources, but it's to your advantage to use your public library with the largest business department. Some university libraries or career counseling departments also have impressive collections of printed and online resources, including Discover, SIGI PLUS, or other career guidance software. These may be helpful, especially as a foundation for further investigation. Keep current with developments in your field by reading business magazines and journals, as well as newspapers.

Talking with knowledgeable people in your area of interest is a wonderful—and fun—way to get the information you need. There is no substitute for that counsel at any stage in your career, as Fred discovered.

When he started his MBA program, Fred thought he wanted a marketing career. By the time he'd finished, he'd grown interested in product development but wasn't sure it would be a good choice for him.

Fred had to talk with product developers in different industries to find out what they did. What skills and experience did they have? How did they become product developers? How has their activity changed since they started? What trends did they see emerging? What about employment prospects? Etc. Etc. Etc. Eventually, Fred found a job doing product development for a packaging company. He's learning by doing.

Job Targeting: An Interim Step

If you're still goal-less despite your best efforts, you may be able to develop a job target as an interim step. A job target is a work direction that is less specific than a goal. A good job target uses your interests, skills, and personal qualities in work that is personally satisfying.

One quick technique you could use to help you focus is to use the classified ads as a resource. Each Sunday for at least three weeks, cut out all the ads that interest you—even if you don't qualify for them. After three weeks, take a look at what you have. Can you see a pattern? Are you surprised at what you see?

If you've clipped ads for pediatric nurse or software developer, explore that field. Talk with people who do that kind of work. You may be surprised to learn that you don't need as much additional education/training as you had assumed. And you'll probably meet some terrific people. You've got a lot to gain. What do you have to lose?

HOW TO REACH YOUR GOAL

Techniques You Can Use[4]

1. Set your goal with a specific time frame. Whether you want to be president of the U.S., executive secretary to the director of the local zoo, or an electronics engineer, you have accomplished something really important by setting your long-range goal.

When will you achieve it? Visions don't become reality overnight. It may take years. Even decades. But you must set a date. Your goal is a dream with a deadline!

- ◆ I will be elected president of the U.S. in 2020.
- ◆ I will become executive secretary to the director of the zoo one year from today (February 2, 19xx).
- ◆ I will graduate with a bachelor's degree in electrical engineering in three years and two months from today, which is March 15, 19xx.

2. Write it. Writing your goal helps you achieve it because it:

- ◆ demonstrates your commitment
   Now you have a signed contract with yourself!
   That's your employment insurance contract.
- ◆ impresses the idea on your subconscious
- ◆ helps to clarify it
- ◆ helps you to prioritize
- ◆ helps you to plan

After you've done this, pat yourself on the back! Only a tiny fraction of the population (some estimate only 1-2%) write their goals.

3. Break down your goal into sub-goals. Once your long-term career goal is set, you can begin planning to achieve it. One useful technique is to break down your goal into shorter-term sub-goals. By using concepts and techniques suggested in this book, you should be able to find employment *consistent with that goal* in 3 months.

Give yourself some leeway and use 6 months as a very workable time frame for achieving your goal. Once your 6-month goal is set, decide on your 2- and 4-month objectives as intermediary steps to help you reach your goal.

Is it fair to use the same time frame for all kinds of jobs? It has been estimated that it takes one month of job hunting for every $10,000 in salary, reflecting the fact that there are fewer high-level jobs, especially as organizational pyramids continue to flatten. But the experience of thousands of job seekers from a wide range of backgrounds strongly indicates that the length of time it takes to find employment depends much more on your attitude and job search skills than on the level of the position you are seeking.

4. Get specific: Create your Goal Setting/Planning Guide. Using the following section as a guide, take a piece of paper and begin to develop your Goal Setting/Planning Guide. At this time, you are focusing on goals. After you have read Chapters 5 and 6, you will be better prepared to develop your action plans. However, if you already know what you have to do, complete the entire Guide now.

Write the goal you think you can achieve 6 months from today. State your goal positively as something you have accomplished. For example:

My 6-Month Goal

The date is:_____(6 months from today).
"I am enjoying my first job as a CPA for Big Six Accounting, earning $35,000 a year."

---

5. Reality check: What are you willing to do to achieve your goal? Is it a goal? Or a fantasy? What are you willing to do? You'd love to be an astronaut or a pharmacist but don't want to go through all the training? Whether it's a goal or a fantasy depends to a remarkable extent on your determination to achieve it. There are, of course, other factors. It's a little late for you to become a child prodigy. But it's not too late for a tremendous number of options. New careers can be started at almost any age, including the so-called retirement years.

GOAL SETTING and PLANNING GUIDE
The more specific you can be, the better.

GOALS:

Long-term goal:

How long will this take?

Immediate Action Plan:
I will obtain employment by:

My position will be:

My target is:
Industry:
Company size:
Location:
Compensation range:
Other factors:

PLANNING:

My action plan is:
  Now-2 months:
  2-4 months:
  4-6 months:
To help me reach this goal:
  I will start doing the following:

  I will stop doing:

Signed: Date:

Look at your goal.

- ◆ Are you enthusiastic?
- ◆ Are you committed?
- ◆ Can you achieve your 6-month goal in 6 months?

Is there additional education or training you should be pursuing now? Would a course in strategic planning help you get that managerial job? Is this the time to complete your college degree?

6. Reinforce your commitment. Now, rewrite your goal on your Goal Setting/Planning Guide and place it where it will do the most good, where you can:

- ◆ *See* it most of the day, at least 3 times a day. The bathroom mirror or the door of the refrigerator is a good place for it.
- ◆ *Read* it every day.
- ◆ *Repeat* it out loud every day. Don't just look at it.

In addition,

- ◆ *Make it public.* The more public you make it, the more likely you are to achieve it. That's part of your commitment.
- ◆ *Avoid negative influences. Some people, even good friends or family members, may subtly undercut your efforts with pessimistic comments. Don't let them discourage you.*

7. Envision achieving your goal. Anything worth having doesn't come easily. It takes commitment and discipline. Why not use all your resources, including your imagination?

Make your goal as *real* and as *visible* as possible. Football and basketball players have a big advantage. Their goals are unmistakable. It's not hard for them to keep their eyes on the basket or the end-zone. But goals in life are usually much less tangible. That's why a picture of your goal or something that symbolizes it *could* help. If a large brick colonial is what you want, why not keep a picture of one where you can *see* it *every day*. You might ask a friend to take a picture of you in front of your dream home.

That technique worked for one Sale to Success graduate who had been unemployed for 4 years. When his job as a marketing manager for an industrial company soured, Gary tried his hand at writing. After two books—but no publisher—he was lonely, dejected, and weary of hearing "When are you going to get a job?"

An antique car buff, Gary kept a picture of a classic Rolls-Royce convertible on his desk as he enrolled in the professional sales training program. Fortified by his newly honed skills, he persuaded PaineWebber to give him a chance.

Within seven years, he reported excitedly, "I drive to work in a Rolls. It's a used one," he confided, "but what a beauty!"

Whether your goal is the grand opening of your restaurant, owning a Rolls-Royce, or becoming a veterinarian, the more you can experience it with all your senses, the more empowering it will be. If you put your imagination to work, rather than depend solely on your will power and determination, you'll probably get better results faster.

Visualization exercises. Most athletes train mentally, as well as physically, because that kind of training has proven effective in achieving top performance. When we see an Olympic diver, concentrating deeply just before his dive, he is performing visually and kinesthetically. He creates in his mind the template of the perfect dive that will guide his real body.[5]

If you're clearly focused on your goals, you can use this same kind of "end-state imagery to imagine yourself in a peak performance state,"[6] successful, and admired. In note 7 in the Notes section at the end of this book are instructions for an exercise in visualization that takes just a few minutes a day. The template in your mind will be an image of yourself not executing a perfect dive but achieving your goal.[7]

8. Build belief. The biggest part of achieving your goal is writing it down. But it is not enough. You must *build belief in yourself. Commit yourself to accomplishing your goal. Commitment is belief that something is attainable through your own efforts.*

Optimists and pessimists are both right. If you think you can, you *can.* If you think you *can't, you* will insure *that* outcome. Since you're insuring yourself, why not go for a positive outcome?

Once you're committed to your goal, you must take charge, develop a positive approach, and plan. Think of yourself as the artist painting your self-portrait 5 or 10 years from now. What you will look like depends on the goals you set, the plans you make, and the action you take to implement them. Will it be a masterpiece? Or a canvas with only a few tentative brush strokes?

EMPLOYMENT INSURANCE CHECKLIST

✓ Did you set your goal?
✓ Is it achievable (but requires you to stretch)?
✓ Is it measurable?
✓ Did you write it?
✓ Did you create your Goal Setting/Planning Guide?
✓ Did you do a reality check?
✓ How committed are you to reaching your goal?
✓ Are you enthusiastic?
✓ How are you reinforcing your commitment?
✓ Do you see, read, and repeat your goal at least 3 times a day?
✓ Have you made it public?
✓ Are you avoiding negative influences that may undercut your efforts?
✓ Can you envision achieving your goal?

CHAPTER 4

❖

Take Charge: Develop a Positive Approach

You've assessed yourself and set your goals. Now you have a better idea of what you can do and what you want to do. But what if no one seems to want that? Job seekers who find few (or no) classified ads for people with their credentials often see that as proof that there are no jobs. But that's not a valid conclusion. Eighty percent of jobs are *not advertised*. Finding no ads for people with your credentials means that:

- ◆ You have to search more creatively—Or
- ◆ It may be time for some new skill development

The latter is always a good idea. You must constantly be learning and upgrading your skills, and you're never too old for that. But what is needed now is more likely to be the former—more and better searching. To do that, you're reframing yourself, taking charge and developing a positive, enterprising approach.

WHAT DOES TAKING CHARGE MEAN?

Entrepreneurial Options

Being self-employed means, simply, that you're open *for* business. And *to* business. That you're receptive to new ideas, and, even more, that you're searching for them and emerging opportunities. It certainly does not mean that you must set up a shop of some kind, selling office furniture or custom-

tailored balloons. There are many different ways to use the entrepreneurial approach:

1. As a transition to a full-time job, possibly as an interim position.
2. As your new business. The business could take various shapes. For example:

   ♦ You could provide services to many clients/customers or to 4 or 5 "anchor" clients on an ongoing basis. These clients may not want a full-time employee benefits person (or purchaser or computer trainer). But they may need you for 8, 10, or 15 hours a week. Many former managers, especially those with about 20 years of experience, are developing this kind of business.

   ♦ You could function as a consultant, offering solutions to problems.

   ♦ Or you may want to be a temporary executive, not only offering solutions but also implementing them.

There should be no conflict between doing consulting work and searching for a job. Unfortunately, some people seem to create conflict by putting the two activities into separate boxes in their heads. That's what Martin, a 52-year-old former executive, did. He became a financial consultant after his job search foundered. For three years, he had mailed out many hundreds of resumes. The result? Only a handful of meetings with hiring authorities. And no offers.

"I don't have time to look for a job," he complained, "because I'm always busy with these short-term assignments."

In the interim, his marriage of 26 years had deteriorated badly because his wife didn't think he was trying hard enough to find a job. Remarkably, Martin had failed to see every one of these short-term assignments as an opportunity for something more. He never tried to convert any of them into longer-range assignments or full-time jobs. More than one-third of temporary jobs become permanent, but temporary employment agencies have no lock on the "temp to perm" concept. You can do that yourself.

And, when you're self-employed, you *have* to do it yourself. That's the only way to survive. You are, after all, the president of your own service company. You know what services you can offer, what you are selling. To launch your service business, you have to find out who needs it and how you can reach them. These are the basic questions any businessperson or job seeker needs to ask—and answer.

Find a Need and Fill It

And if you cannot find a need, create it. That's the entrepreneur's credo. Ask your potential customers what they want. Then, if it's something you can do, do it. And do it well. If it's not something you can do, move on to the next potential buyer. Whatever your career objective—a job, a career change, or self-employment, you can use the entrepreneurial approach.

That's what Sam did. After spending all his working life in freight management, Sam was in his mid-fifties when the company he had been working for went out of business. Reeling from deregulation and the decline in manufacturing, the trucking industry was skidding downhill. Jobs in operations management—the kind of work Sam did so well—were gone.

But that didn't stop him. Sam called on former business associates in the freight-handling business and asked what *they* needed. It wasn't operations management. It was sales. And they wanted someone with previous sales experience.

"These people knew me as an operations guy—on the loading dock. Giving orders. Now I had to persuade them that I could sell. They had to see me in a new light." To do that, Sam drew on his former sales experience, asked questions, listened, and was hired. That was 1988. "Sales was the doorway to my company. I did sales for about 3 years and gradually, the president has given me more and more responsibilities."

The smile in his voice speaks volumes. Sam is living proof that finding a need and filling it is what employment, as well as entrepreneurship, is all about.

You Can Cover the Business Beat

In searching for your job, you're probing for information like an investigative reporter. What qualities do you need to succeed?

According to Scott Simon and Ray Suarez, two award-winning reporters for National Public Radio, the most important quality is curiosity—"a consuming form of curiosity," says Suarez.[1] Simon adds, "Perseverance is a fine trait in a reporter," a point echoed by a Cleveland *Plain Dealer* business editor, Mary Ellen Crowley Huesken. "Persistence is number one," observed Huesken:

> "A good reporter must also be creative in terms of making connections. For example, if something's happening to one person, maybe it's happening to others. Good reporters are also *open* to information which may not be what they expected. If that is very interesting, they have to be flexible enough to pursue it.
>
> "Business reporters talk to as many people as possible to find out *what* they know and *who* they know to get more information," she added. "They keep in

touch with people on their beat to find out what's happening. If the reporter who covers law firms, for instance, finds out that one firm hired a person to do nothing but public relations, she might ask: Is this a trend?"[2]

The Art of Asking Questions

Job seekers should be asking the same kinds of questions. You are entrepreneurs, explorers, private detectives, researchers all in one. Curious. Open to information that may not be what you expected. Probe below the surface. The treasures you'll uncover are unmet needs in the marketplace. Most of them will not come neatly wrapped in newspaper articles. If you don't actively search for them, you could be looking right past them.

The art of asking questions is almost overlooked in our society. In communications, the spotlight is on speaking, the theater of presenting. The ability to ask good questions—*and listen to the answers*—is almost ignored. These skills don't have much pizzazz. But they're essential in persuasion. And in finding employment.

Asking questions in a nonthreatening, nonchallenging way is an art. You will, of course, invariably be diplomatic and avoid any hint of "grilling" the other person. (For more about the questioning process, see Chapter 14.)

Use the Information You Get

By asking questions, you'll undoubtedly be able to uncover needs. *Filling them* is something else. How will you use the information you obtain?

The entrepreneurial role is probably the best one to bridge the gap between information and employment. Employers want results. You may be able to help meet their needs in your area of expertise, whether it's operations, materials handling, or trust services. Regardless of what you have to offer, the only way you will know if you can be helpful is to meet them, exchange ideas, and explain how you can benefit them.

REFRAME THE JOB MARKET

Where Can You Be Entrepreneurial?

Everywhere! Explore your universe! Expand it! You don't have to launch a space station to do that. Discovery happens when you're curious. Treasure-hunt right in your neighborhood. There could be gold within a few miles, right in those office complexes, restaurants, and shopping malls. To find it, keep digging. What kind of business is this? Who owns it? What do they do here? Where do these products come from? Who do they sell to? Is this a franchise? Part of a national/international business? Who manages this property? If you keep digging, you'll eventually hit pay dirt.

All the world's a stage, said the Bard, and technology has greatly expanded the theater. So has reframing. Shopping centers are now entertainment complexes. Even supermarkets are show biz. Sideshows for kids have become routine. Some markets offer massages. Others feature singles nights and cooking classes. At least one caters benefit parties for PTAs and other nonprofits after hours on Sundays. The opportunities for reframing are endless.

Conferences, trade and professional association meetings, business and trade shows are great places to see what's going on. Who's in business? What are they doing? And how? Have you ever gone to a business show in an industry different from your own? A graphics show? Or a computer show? You might easily meet the head of the company. If they're typical small businesspeople, they're proud of their business and would love to talk about it. Think of all the growing businesses represented at shows that need people with your skills—in accounting, systems analysis, public relations, marketing, etc.

Business shows are noisy and hectic. You may not love them. But you don't have to marry them. Just get information. And business cards. As you collect them, make some appropriate notes to help you when you follow up.

Then do it. Call and set up appointments. By following up on your initial meeting, you've done much more than accomplish objective #1: meeting the hiring authority. You also have some information about what they do, how they market, and who they hire. You're already *inside* the organization! Now why not ask for a tour of their facility? That's an invaluable opportunity to learn about them, ask questions, and possibly make some helpful suggestions. That could be the launching pad for your new job.

Being entrepreneurial does not mean that job fairs and other traditional vehicles for finding employment should be overlooked. They can be useful, of course, but they should not be relied on as the best or only way to find your job. There are, obviously, many more creative ways to do that.

The Only Certainty Is Change

In the life of an organization, change is constant. Mergers, acquisitions, new products and techniques transform organizations at an ever-increasing pace. Turnover averages about 20% a year. Every change generates opportunities. And needs. Whatever the size of the organization, it is probably safe to assume that there are unmet needs, although there may be no official job openings.

Increasingly, corporations hire professionals and others on a temporary or contract basis. Engineers have been employed on a project basis for many years. Now, everyone "temps." Massive downsizing has produced a new class of corporate itinerants: lawyers, human resource professionals, chief financial officers, and even chief operating officers. The term you use—interim executives or executive migrant workers—probably reflects your attitude about this phenomenon.

The entrepreneurial approach is based, in part, on the following apparent realities:

1. There are more unmet organizational needs than jobs.
2. Each unmet need represents an opportunity for employment.
3. These opportunities exist in companies of all sizes.
4. These opportunities exist in all economic conditions ("bad" as well as "good" times).

Timing It Right!

Ideally, you'll arrive on the scene to provide your services just in time. A need exists but an opening has not yet been created. That happens every day. Just think about your own experiences in the hiring process. I have asked hundreds of people who have hired personnel:

Q. How long did it take for a hiring decision to be made in your organization?

Here are some typical responses:

A. It could be a few months to get all the approvals. A few weeks at least.
It depended on how badly we needed that person. Sometimes it took years.

Q. How would you feel if someone with very appropriate credentials called during that period and asked for a meeting?

A. It would seem like they were reading our minds. I'm sure we would have seen him!

Q. Would that job seeker have an advantage over others who might apply?

A. Of course!

Q. Why?

A. If he's right there as the job is being developed, he could help shape it. He becomes an *insider* and probably has a better shot at that job than anyone else.

That was precisely what happened to Charles, an industrial engineer. A Sale to Success participant, he was making "cold" calls to potential employers, including BP America. His call to the head of the industrial engineering department came right after a staff meeting ended. A decision had just been made: They needed another industrial engineer. The timing was perfect. Because Charles was brought in as a temporary employee, normal hiring practices were dispensed with. Charles got his job. And like many "temp" positions, it lasted for many years.

Timing it *right* sounds like luck. Sometimes it is. More often, though, it's the result of persistence. You can create your good luck by making enough calls to hiring authorities.

People, Not Organizations, Hire

Charles's story makes another significant point. People, not organizations, hire. Charles had taken the initiative and called the decision maker. Had he gone the traditional route and contacted the human resources department, he would have been told, correctly, that there were no openings. The *opening* in this huge, multinational firm had *closed* before human resources even knew about it!

How Can You Benefit from the Entrepreneurial Approach?

The logic for the entrepreneurial approach is compelling. By thinking and functioning as though you're self-employed, you'll greatly expand your opportunities. And you'll be more relaxed. Traditional job seekers are typically anxious about their job search because so much seems to be riding on each call, each letter, each meeting.

The result? Sweaty palms!

The entrepreneurial approach is less stressful. Your eggs are not all in one full-time job basket. Each contact represents an opportunity—not the *make* or *break* for your entire future. You'll recognize at the outset that most contacts will not produce business. But if you make *enough* calls, you *will* generate business!

The entrepreneurial approach helps you to:

- ◆ Maintain control over your employment future
- ◆ Feel better about yourself (as a result)
- ◆ Feel positive because you're using your skills
- ◆ Learn new skills, expand your horizons
- ◆ Interact with others as a businessperson

- Earn some income
- Show many people what you can do
- Provide an audition for a full-time position.
- Showcase your entrepreneurial skills, confidence, and ability to take risks. These are much in demand in the corporate community.

And the entrepreneurial approach works! It has been highly effective for job seekers for more than 10 years, including periods of double-digit unemployment.

The New Security

A full-time position with a solid company, complete with a good benefits package, is the definition of security that many of us grew up with. And that's probably what you're looking for. But as Harvard Business School professor Rosabeth Moss Kanter observed: "If your security no longer comes from being *employed*, then it must come from being *employable*."[3] And from being able to market yourself. When America's most paternalistic companies lay off tens of thousands of workers, it's clear that security is not something we can expect from employers.

You are your own security. It consists of your skills and your ability to market them. Being self-employed and self-insured may be more self-reliance than you really want. But since it's clearly a practical response to current realities, let's focus on the opportunities it offers and take advantage of them. Planning will help to insure that your voyage of discovery is as smooth as possible. That's what the next chapter is about.

EMPLOYMENT INSURANCE CHECKLIST

✓ Are you ready to take charge and be entrepreneurial?
✓ Can you function like an investigative reporter in a nonthreatening way?
✓ Are you asking enough people for information?
✓ Are you curious?
✓ Are you persistent?
✓ Are you exploring opportunities everywhere, including your area?
✓ Are you going to trade and professional conferences, meetings, business and industry shows?
✓ Are you finding needs that you can fill?

CHAPTER 5

❖

Planning: Making Dreams Come True

WHY PLAN?

"People get addicted to planning because it makes dreams come true."[1] The more important your goal, the more vital is the planning process. What is more significant than your future?

Planning Works

Failing to plan doesn't guarantee failure, but it fosters a seat-of-the-pants approach that tends to squander your precious resources, like time, energy, and, ultimately, money. Planning makes so much sense that almost everyone would do it if they really thought about it. And knew how to do it. But many people don't. Fifty-four percent of our survey respondents indicated that they had no plan to find employment.

Planning works because it structures your ideas, time, and efforts. You benefit because you:

- save a great deal of time
- gain a sense of control (of your day and yourself)
- gain confidence.

Specifically, planning:[2]

- provides direction and focus
- helps you to set priorities
- helps you to proceed *systematically*
- includes developing strategies to accomplish goals
- makes it easier to break down your goal into achievable parts
- makes it easier to measure progress

◆ gives you something to return to when you get sidetracked. If you have no plan, there is no way to get back on track.

Your Marketing Plan

As you know, the kind of plan which is particularly relevant to your needs is a marketing plan.

> **"Whether you're in business or seeking a job,**
> **the key to success is**
> **understanding what you're selling,**
> **who needs it**
> **and how you're going to reach them:**
> **the marketing plan."**[3]

Having assessed yourself and set your goal, you know what you're selling—from your perspective. To communicate that effectively, you have to understand the prospective employer's point of view.

What Are You Selling?

Yourself, of course. And you know that you have fine skills, talents, and a lot of energy to offer an employer. But that, unfortunately, isn't sufficient. Your success will depend, to a great extent, on your ability to present yourself in a professional manner.

PLAN TO COMMUNICATE EFFECTIVELY

Avoid Common Pitfalls

Every job seeker is, of course, eager to land a good job with a good organization, opportunities for growth, good salary, convenient location, etc. Some people are so preoccupied with their needs, however, that they actually undercut their own efforts. The results might be amusing if they weren't so sad.

Being excessively "me" oriented is a common pitfall. One example was a middle-aged man who applied for a position on my staff some years ago. When I inquired about his qualifications, he responded: "I live right around the corner." "What difference does that make?" I asked. He thought for a while and replied: "Well, I won't have any trouble getting here in the winter."

Another example was the resume of a young college graduate, a computer science major, which stated:

> Objective: A position where I will be able to contribut (the final "e" was omitted) my skills in software design and *which will allow me to attend graduate school in computer science.* [My italics].

Although his skills were much in demand, the young man had received no positive responses from the dozens of software companies he had contacted. No wonder! The glaring typo at the beginning of his resume communicated unacceptable carelessness. Even more inappropriate was his statement about what he expected the company to do *for him.* Being trained to do the job the way the organization wants is, of course, standard procedure. But discussions about *their* advancing *your* education should be initiated only after you have accepted their job offer *at the earliest.*

Describing your qualifications in meaningless generalities is another common pitfall. What you're selling must be of value to the other person. Job seekers who don't plan what they're going to say are apt to mutter such vacuous statements as:

"I'm a good team player."

"I'm a good communicator."

"I like people." (Do you know anyone who claims *not* to like people?)

The most common error, however, is **making too many assumptions.** Job seekers assume that prospective employers will know how valuable they are because of their titles, degrees, and years of experience.

"I was the operations manager for 14 years with the Wormy Compost Corporation and was recruited by MooseMoss of America to run their operations

department. I was there for 6 years when they moved all their corporate functions out of state. My family didn't want to move, so here I am."

OR

"I have a BS from State University. I started working for the Crabgrass Corporation in marketing right after graduation. I did crabgrass and dandelion marketing for 8 years, but the last few years were really bad for crabgrass. The company went Chapter 11 in November."

The "So What? Machine"

Imagine that on every employer's head is a *So What?* machine. It's like a toaster, except that it beeps and flashes red lights. Every time you make a statement about yourself, like: "I graduated from State U. in 1979" or "I like people," a *So What?* sign pops up like a piece of burnt toast. *What difference does it make—TO THEM?*

S O   W H A T   ? ? ?

Make It Perfectly Clear

When you say "I like people," you undoubtedly think everyone knows what you mean. It's obvious, isn't it? You get along well with your boss and co-workers. You're not a troublemaker. That should be a reason for hiring you, right?

Not if "I like people" means something completely different to them. The last time they hired a really friendly type, he spent all day at the coffee machine, rerunning his favorite team's plays while everyone's work stacked up. Now when the company recruits, they seek out hermits!

If you're an agreeable person who is great at creating a harmonious atmosphere, why not say that? Your interpersonal skills could be the reason you're hired—especially if you find out that this particular department has been plagued with friction. What they really need is a gentle, soothing person like you.

Most job seekers rattle off facts about themselves, assuming that others will understand the significance of what they're saying. But what does

14 years of accounting experience mean? It *could* mean that you saved the company megabucks by initiating cost-effective procedures. But it could also mean that you learned the job in 6 months and coasted for 13 1/2 years!

Emphasize Benefits

You're looking at the "product" (yourself) from the "customer's" (hiring authority's) point of view, and asking:

- What are my particular skills and abilities that bring added value?
- What distinguishes me from other suppliers (job seekers)?
- **Why should they buy my services (hire me)?**

People buy because they have a real or perceived need of some kind. They want to gain in some way. They are buying benefits that they believe will contribute to their well-being.

It's not your 8 years of experience in sports marketing. Or your MBA. You're selling your ability to satisfy their needs and wants through your services. To benefit the individual decision maker and the organization. What value or satisfaction can you add? Essentially, these are bottom-line considerations.[4] Can you:

- increase good things: profits, prestige, image, safety, efficiency, quality, well-being, security, comfort, convenience?
- decrease or avoid distasteful things: costs, time, loss, pain, anxiety, hassles, competition?

Some of these benefits, like profits, can be quantified. Others, like prestige, image, pain, and anxiety, are subjective and not easily measured. But they are no less important. The most powerful presentations include both emotional *and* factual appeals. That's because even the most hardheaded among us often make decisions *emotionally* and then justify them logically.

That's the way you buy, isn't it? You buy a new suit because it makes you look good and feel good, not because it provides simple protection from the elements or is the cheapest suit you can find. Some car buyers claim that all they want is basic transportation, but they choose red or black cars because they're "in." The added comfort—and prestige—of the luxury sedan justify the higher cost for certain drivers because they add value.

When an employer hires an experienced supervisor rather than a novice who would work for much less, he might say he's paying for 11 years of experience. But he's really buying comfort and security, believing that she'll do the job right and not mess up. By paying more, he's getting more. He's buying "insurance."

Keep this in mind when you have a job offer and prepare for salary negotiations. Like everybody else, employers want to get the most for their money. But the lowest price is not necessarily the best value *for them*. They may be able to hire another production controller or head of nursing for less money. But will they feel as secure about that decision as when they offer that job to you? Not if you've translated facts about yourself into benefits for them!

If you're young and don't have much experience, what you're selling, essentially, is your potential—your youth, your energy, your trainability. And you're cheap! You're always selling what you honestly have.

Develop a "Them" Orientation

Wouldn't it be great if your skills and abilities were in such demand that employers lined up to get your autograph? The superstars who are in that enviable position are there because they are very attuned to their audiences (customers or clients). Their success depends on providing what *others* want and value.

To understand precisely what you're selling means understanding exactly what they're willing to buy. And why. No one sells in a vacuum, as we'll explore more fully in the next chapter. You know your goal and what you have to offer. But it may not be exactly what they want to buy right now. Negotiating the difference is the art of finding employment.

Sometimes, the gap is minimal. That was Jennifer's situation. She was discouraged when her fresh university degree in interior design and her impressive portfolio were not generating any job offers. Hiring authorities were insisting that their entry-level people have CAD-CAM training. It was a small but significant lack in Jennifer's education. She heard what the marketplace was telling her and enrolled in a CAD-CAM course at a local community college. Within weeks, she was hired by a well-respected architecture firm.

Listen to the Marketplace

The gap between what you're selling and what they'll buy may be larger, requiring you to be more flexible and creative. Fortunately, you have the capacity to adapt what you are selling. To emphasize certain skills and abilities—and learn new ones. That's why selling your services is different from selling other products. They can't change. Your sofa can be used in different ways, but it can't become a refrigerator.

What is the marketplace telling you? Whether you're a washing machine repair person or an aerospace engineer, you can transfer your abilities to diagnose, fix, and design many more things than washing machines and planes.

Make Them Feel Comfortable with You

You must realize that your next employer, like everyone else who buys something—especially a major purchase—has a lot of doubt. She needs to be reassured. You must help her overcome her fear of high pressure, uncertainty about you and your motives (are you merely interested in yourself?), and doubt about her decision to employ you. What will her associates think of her decision? Will they approve? Could she get someone else for less? Would it be better to wait?

Take Off Your Shoes!

That's the best way to look for a job! Put on a pair of wingtips! Or whatever *they* are wearing. Look at yourself from *their* perspective.

Job seekers. Ask not what an employer can do for you. Ask what you can do for an employer!

Forgive this appropriation of President Kennedy's eloquent appeal. But it is an important point. Ask yourself: Why should they hire you? What can you do for them?

MAKE IT EASY FOR THEM TO UNDERSTAND

Your ability to benefit your employer is why they *should* hire you. When you communicate that powerfully, they *will* hire you! To do that:

- ◆ Describe clearly what you *have* done
- ◆ Provide evidence for your claims
- ◆ Explain *what you can do for them*
- ◆ Clarify *why they should hire you*

Use Mini-Stories[5]

Remember the achievements you listed in your self-assessment? By using what is called the PAR formula, a simple way to help you analyze and explain your accomplishments, you can translate your achievements into succinct little stories. These mini-stories are effective because they tell what you did in a short, clear, memorable way.

P = Problem. What is the problem or situation you faced?

A = Action. What action did you take to resolve it? Why did you do that?

R = Results. What were the results? *Measurable* results are most impressive.

Examples:

Problem: The benefits manager of an insurance brokerage firm faced 20-30% annual increases in the costs of health care benefits for the company's 1,500 employees.

Action: She gathered information and analyzed many options. Then she developed and installed a flexible benefits program and managed a comprehensive communications campaign for employees.

Results: She saved the company approximately $700,000 annually while improving the benefits options available for employees.

Problem: The chief financial officer for a business journal publishing company recognized that prepress expenses were too high.

Action: He isolated author alteration charges and limited the use of traps, screens, and tints.

Results: Prepress expenses were reduced by 45% while the good appearance of the magazines was retained.

Sometimes, you cannot claim the credit you deserve for an accomplishment and it cannot be quantified because you don't have access to the information. That's often the case when you're hired as a "temp" to do a specific project.

Example:

Problem: A major medical school's in-house medical programs were poorly organized and, by their description, "messy." They needed to be debugged and properly organized. A temporary computer programmer was hired, given minimal guidance, and assigned to fix it.

Action: Working alone, she studied the software manual.

Results: She debugged the program and got it functioning properly, completing the assignment by deadline.

The solution is, obviously, to get as much information as you can while you are working—even though it may be a short-term assignment—so that you can document your accomplishments in the future.

What About the Fish That Got Away?

Although you did a great job, you might not have the results to prove it because of circumstances beyond your control. Your work was, nevertheless, impressive—a credit to you and your organization.

Problem: Eileen's environmental consulting company wanted to bid on a $2-million recycling program for New York City. Proposals were due in 10 weeks, a very short time for such a large project.

Action: Eileen quickly consulted with others in-house, developed an approach, and outlined the proposal and budget. She then contacted and obtained the cooperation of 6 appropriate out-of-state subcontractors for specialized parts of the proposal. Overseeing their proposal writing and completing the final, multifaceted package required a monumental effort on Eileen's part.

Result: A splendid proposal, which enhanced her company's prestige and credibility, was submitted on time. Although they didn't win this contract, officials at Eileen's company stated that her proposal contributed indirectly to their success in obtaining another contract from New York City a few months later.

Mini-Story Tips[6]

- ◆ Keep it short. Thirty seconds should be enough. You can elaborate later in response to their questions.
- ◆ Keep it simple. Avoid confusing the listener with complexities or multiple stories.
- ◆ Be specific and accurate. Use numbers whenever possible. For example, "The procedure I recommended saved them $150,000 a year and they're still using it."
- ◆ Use dollar amounts when talking with a smaller company; percentages are usually more impressive to larger organizations.
- ◆ Use action words to describe how you solved the problem(s)—you created, initiated, proposed, etc.
- ◆ Never exaggerate. When in doubt, *under*state. Your credibility will be enhanced if you err on the side of caution.

◆ Give yourself credit for what you (not the others) did. "I" (not "we") "proposed changing the operation so that we saved 45% of the raw materials. That meant $60,000 in savings for that component alone."

Your Turn: Write Your Mini-Stories

Take a sheet of paper and use the PAR formula to write *several* of your accomplishments clearly and succinctly.

MY ACCOMPLISHMENTS

Problem:
Action:
Results:

When you do a good job of describing your past achievements, potential employers will be impressed that:

◆ you are a good problem solver
◆ you are results oriented
◆ you can organize your thoughts and express yourself well
◆ your story shows something positive about you: your dedication, good follow-through, etc.

Are You Keeping Your Achievements a Secret?

After helping clients recognize the substantial contributions they have made to their previous employers, I scan their resumes. Although they are often prepared by professional resume services, the job seekers' accomplishments—what employers are looking for—are frequently buried or missing completely!

Your achievements are important. Why not highlight them? They not only communicate what you have done—and suggest what you can do. They can also help to identify you, not only in your resume, but in "sound bites." These are short, memorable messages you can use to introduce yourself in person and in writing. For example, Paul, the truck stop manager, had business cards printed with his name, address, phone number, and

Saved MegaOil Inc. more than $750,000
while improving customer service.

Within two weeks, he was hired!

When you use your sound bite in face-to-face situations, remember that the effectiveness of what you're communicating depends more on your body language and tone of voice than on the actual words. Be sure you are positive and upbeat. Introduce yourself confidently and with good humor.

Instead of:

"I worked for the Fatty Fitness Club until they eliminated my job in May."

(which will elicit an "Oh, what a shame" response, an embarrassed pause, then a quick change of subject), why not say:

"I helped increase our fitness club membership 18% in the last two years!"

(Now they'll want to know **what** you did and **how** you did it.)

"While I was the national supplier of duct tape for Fly-by-Night Airlines, we sold their mechanics 20% more duct tape every year for seven years."

"My clients at Pork Barrel Political Consulting wrote dozens of letters expressing their appreciation for my services when they heard there was less pork around and I might leave."

"Sam Shotty, my boss at Shotty Security Services, told me I was the best trouble shooter Shotty's ever had—and he's been in business 23 years!"

Translate Facts About Yourself into Benefits for Your Next Employers[7]

Fact	Accomplishment	Benefit
good student	graduated top 20% of class	quick study, save training costs
worked summers	paid 75% of college expenses	industrious, increase efficiency
management trainee, fast food chain	completed management training program	management potential save time, money
communications major	edited campus newsletter	improve quality, reduce costs of corporate communications

How Can You Benefit Your Next Employer?

For each of the facts you have written about yourself, you should be able to list at least one benefit to prospective employers. These are usually bottom-line benefits. Using the format below, take some paper and write at least 5 benefits that you can bring to an employer. These are, in fact, 5 reasons why they should hire you.

Why They Should Hire Me		
Facts	*Accomplishments*	*Benefits*

How you can benefit your next employer and why they should hire you are key points in your marketing efforts. You'll be reviewing these and your other worksheets when you write your resume and letters, as described in Chapters 8 and 9.

PLAN TO HAVE GOOD REFERENCES

Good References = More Employment Insurance

You're not the only one communicating about what you have to offer. References can *make* or *break* you. If you're just starting out and have no work experience, ask your teachers, your minister or rabbi, or business-people who know you to write letters for you. Internships, unpaid if necessary, will give you invaluable work experience, as well as references. Even if your job is part-time and temporary, don't hesitate to ask your supervisor(s) for letters of reference. The more the merrier.

Reference Rule: Don't leave any employment without at least one reference letter.

The people you ask will usually say they'd be glad to be a reference for you. That's wonderful. But you don't know whether they'll be there when you need them. With so much job changing and moving, your best bet is to have their reference letter on the company letterhead now.

Be empathetic and make it easy for them. Tell them you know how rushed they are right now and ask if it would help if you drafted a letter, outlining your responsibilities and accomplishments. When you do, there's a good chance that they'll have it typed on the company's letter-head. And you'll have some additional employment insurance.

Your References: Key Players on Your Team

Much more impressive, of course, is a personal contact from your reference to your prospective employer. That call or letter can be a powerful introduction or follow-up to your meeting with the decision maker. If she's someone the hiring authority knows and respects, her comments could easily tilt the decision in your favor.

Nurture your relationships with your references so they'll continue to be your advocates. Always ask their permission before using their names and be sure they have current, relevant information about you. Whenever possible, give them the names of the people who will be contacting them, as well as the title and major responsibilities of the position(s) you are seeking. Keeping them informed, thanking them for their help each time, and doing something for them will help maintain strong bonds.

How Can You Smooth Over Unfriendly Departures?

You will, of course, always try to end every relationship amicably, but that's not always easy. If you were dismissed from your job, you may be feeling angry and hurt. It's to your advantage, however, to get your letter of reference *immediately*.

If you've already left, make an appointment with your former boss right away. You know that one poor reference could jeopardize your future, so take the initiative. Call and ask: What can I honestly tell prospective employers about why I was let go?[8] Be sure your stories are consistent. You can probably agree that it was a difference in management philosophy or something like that.

Remember that you have the most to lose by letting a bad situation fester. You're negotiating as a mature, independent person who wants to set the record straight and move on. If your approach is calm and nonaccusatory, they'll probably understand that you need to work and won't stand in your way.

Your Business Associates Can Be Great References Too!

Former employers are not, of course, the only—or even the best—references for you. Others, like clients, customers, and suppliers with whom you worked closely, can be very valuable, especially if your former boss is not inclined to be effusive—or company policy doesn't allow her to be.

Jane, a young woman with a flair for flowers and a commitment to customer service, was thinking entrepreneurially when she asked her regular customers for brief statements about her service. She compiled those testimonials, which praised her warmly for her originality and dedication, on three attractively formatted pages. Within weeks, she was hired as a manager by a gift shop chain owner who was impressed by her enterprise, as well as her talents with flowers and customers.

SELF-KNOWLEDGE REVISITED

You have begun the learning experience of your life, assessing yourself and setting your goals. Self-knowledge, as the ancient Greeks recognized, is the beginning of all knowledge. Simultaneously, you have been asking—and answering—the first question in your marketing plan: what am I selling? In this chapter, the focus has been on planning how to communicate what you have to offer. Being sensitive to the employers' perspective is a major consideration here. You're asking: Why should they hire me?

The questions raised in these first chapters are probably the most difficult you'll encounter in your job search. They go to the heart of who you are and what you want to do with your life. Many job seekers bypass these issues. You will, hopefully, continue to explore those questions as you move ahead to the next section and ask the second question in your marketing plan: Who needs it?

EMPLOYMENT INSURANCE CHECKLIST

✓ Are you empathetic? Can you put yourself in their shoes?
✓ Do you know why they should hire you?
✓ Do you know what you can do for them?

✓ Are you keeping your achievements a secret?
✓ Are you using the PAR formula to describe your accomplishments effectively?
✓ Can you explain how you will benefit your next employer?
✓ Do you have references from every job?
✓ Are your references strong advocates for you?
✓ Is your explanation for your departure consistent with your former employer's?

CHAPTER 6

❖

Prior Proper Planning
Prevents Perpetually
Poor Performance[1]

Who needs it? That's the second question in your marketing plan and the focus of this chapter. To answer that question, you're in the second phase of your job search: learning about *them*, the employers, the industry, companies, and decision makers. That's a lot of information to acquire quickly, so you'll want to plan to make the best use of your time and energy. Planning doesn't insure success but prior proper planning prevents perpetually poor performance.

WHO NEEDS WHAT YOU'RE OFFERING?

Who Is Your Ideal Customer?

Now that you're thinking entrepreneurially, you know that there are many more needs for your services than just "openings." One way to discover *who needs it* is to start by describing your ideal customer (employer) in terms of the:

- type of organization
- size
- location, etc.[2]

Additional Questions You'll Want to Ask

- How many customers are there?
- Why would they buy your product/services?
- Why would they *not* buy your product/services?
- What other kinds of customers do you have?

To target your market, you'll be:

- researching organizations which are potential buyers of your services
- prioritizing them into A, B, and C companies
- contacting them to learn more about their needs

Develop a List

After some preliminary research, you can probably develop a list of organizations that may be able to use your services. Only after you have talked with them, however, will you know if they can benefit from what you offer.

Advertised Positions

The obvious place to look for organizations that need your services is classified advertisements. In addition to your local newspapers, the *Wall Street Journal*, the *New York Times*, and the *National Business Employment Weekly* list openings that may interest you. Major libraries have these and other out-of-town newspapers and may also subscribe to Help Wanted U.S.A., which reproduces on microfiche classified ads from Sunday newspapers in 64 cities. In certain fields, specific journals or other publications that are widely read carry advertisements for their particular professions, industries, and trades.

With a PC and modem, you can find classified ads on job bulletin boards through the Internet and through various commercial databases. The job postings include federal jobs, as well as openings listed by city, state, region, and type of position, like systems analyst.

Although only about 20 percent of jobs are filled through classified ads, they are your best guide to your local market and an important resource. Ignoring them is as unwise as relying on them exclusively. Usually, companies that advertise are inundated with resumes and the competition is awesome. But someone gets those jobs. Why not you?

Classified ads give you a good idea of what employers are looking for, as well as the names of new positions, emerging companies, companies that are moving to your area, etc.

Internal advertising is another valuable source of information, one that's usually overlooked by those outside the organization. Typically, job openings are posted on company bulletin boards (physical and E-mail), newsletters, etc. When you're talking with friends who work for other organizations, why not ask them what kinds of jobs are posted at their companies. They may know you as a wonderful dietitian or nurse and had no idea you were thinking about changing careers. Just knowing what their companies are looking for could help you consider new options and clarify your goals. Of course, if your friends know what you're looking for, they're in a much better position to help you find it.

RESEARCHING WHO NEEDS IT

Take Advantage of Marvelous Resources

Advertised and posted positions are fine, but limited. To get to 80% of the opportunities that are out there, you'll have to move beyond the ads and be more enterprising. Fortunately, there are amazing resources, both impersonal and personal, that you can tap into, including:

- ◆ published and online information from non-company resources.
- ◆ the organization and its employees
- ◆ customers, suppliers, and others who do business with the company

Library Resources

Libraries, especially larger business departments of public libraries, as well as your PC, are treasuries of information. Befriend those wonderful, resourceful people—reference librarians. They'll be happy to help you research specific companies or an entire industry, especially if you avoid their busiest hours: late afternoons and weekends.

If you don't know the 4-digit Standard Industrial Classification (SIC) number which identifies your industry or field of economic activity, you can get that SIC number from the Standard Industrial Code Manual. Or ask the librarian. Once you know this number, you can compile a list of potential employers.

If you are looking for an industry overview, try the *U.S. Industrial Outlook*, published by the U.S. Department of Commerce, which provides forecasts for selected manufacturing and service industries. Standard and Poor's Industry Surveys, which are published quarterly and updated more frequently, may have more useful information.

For basic facts about public and privately held companies, try the massive Dun and Bradstreet directories. Standard and Poor's and Moody's directories provide information, including important financial data, on publicly held companies. National trade journals and directories, as well as professional association publications, are also valuable resources. Look for the special industry overview issues, which are usually published annually.

Additional information is available through the *Wall Street Journal* as well as local newspapers and business magazines. Ask the librarian for the indexes to these publications. If you haven't been keeping up with relevant news, now's the time to do that.

Tap into Online Information Services

Get acquainted with your library's online and CD-ROM database, as well as printed materials. Business InfoTrac is a terrific online system that contains information on 100,000 U.S. corporations, mostly privately held. You don't have to be a computer whiz to use this and, of course, you can always ask the librarian for help. Just type in the name of the company you're researching and you can get key facts about the organization as well as recent articles about the company. Abstracts or entire texts of those articles are available through Business InfoTrac.

InfoTrac's General BusinessFile also provides basic facts about publicly held as well as some private companies. Financial information about certain corporations is also available through Investext on InfoTrac.

Large publicly held corporations are easy to research. Call the company and ask for their annual report and other printed material. Annual reports, required of publicly held companies, contain loads of golden nuggets: names of officers, financial data, products, major accomplishments, and projections for the future. You can also request 10-K reports, which have some of the same information as the annual reports. These 10-K reports may also be available on CD-ROM or microfiche at your library, through the Internet, or various commercial databases.

Smaller companies, which are generating so many new jobs, present more of a challenge. State and local directories, including your local chamber of commerce's membership directory, have the basic facts. You may also find smaller companies in Business InfoTrac and Dun and Bradstreet directories. Some of Dun's specialized, regional, and even national directories list quite a few smaller companies. For information about high-tech companies, try the multivolume Corporate Technology Directory, which also describes their online services.

Libraries and your PC are invaluable resources, but there are other creative ways to get the information you need.

Are You Wearing Your Sherlock Holmes Hat?

Being fully alert to the opportunities that are out there may require a slight change in your behavior. Anne, a customer service manager for a major health insurer in Ohio, explains how she did that when she was looking for a job.

> *"I refocused my reading. When I read the daily paper and the weekly business magazines, I read them from a different perspective. I looked at each article and asked: What are they telling me about their organization? Is there growth potential?*

> *"One day I read a promotional story in the daily paper about the new executive in my company [the organization she later joined] who had been recruited from out of state. In the article, she listed three major things that she wanted to accomplish in her new position. I wrote her a letter, focusing on those three things, outlining what I had done and how I could help her accomplish her goals. Then I followed up very aggressively. I was really insistent. I thought: What have I got to lose? And I got the job!"*

Creativity and persistence paid off for Anne. She not only found a job, she also transferred her skills successfully from one industry (banking) to another (health insurance).

"I explained that I had transferable skills. My mortgage service experience in the bank involved working with customers. And I had really good managerial experience. So becoming a manager of customer service seemed very appropriate."

Anne created her opportunity in January 1991 when the recession had put thousands of people out of work. The article she described was in Ohio's largest newspaper, with a daily circulation of more than 400,000. *Thousands of job seekers read that newspaper and despaired about their plight. Anne read and saw an opportunity!*

Check every section of your local newspapers, not only the business section. The social pages, for example, might have a story about a fund-raising event for the local hospital chaired by the CEO of your top-priority company. Being aware of her commitment gives you a topic of mutual interest to discuss when you meet. That's a nice icebreaker.

Local business magazines and newspapers often have a section where promotions, new hires, new board memberships, etc., are listed. This kind of information could easily signal opportunities for you. When someone is promoted or changes jobs, who is taking on her old responsibilities? If it is an organization you're interested in, why not write a note congratulating the person who was promoted? Follow up with a call. Get acquainted! Don't expect to find a job at that organization, but your new acquaintance might know about other possibilities.

Personal Resources

People can help fill in the inevitable gaps and make your search more interesting and fun. Some of your best resources are employees and former employees of the company you're researching. Through networking, which is described in the next chapter, you can probably get the names of several relevant people. Calling, meeting, and getting acquainted with these individuals can give you invaluable inside information about the organization, its corporate culture, as well as the hiring authority.

Lawyers, accountants, and bankers—especially those who serve the small business community—are excellent sources of information. They know which companies are expanding, the new directions they are taking, etc. Start with accountants, lawyers, and bankers you know—then network with others.

The company's customers and suppliers are another resource. Let's say you are a public relations specialist with expertise in consumer products. You have identified a successful hair care products company as an ideal organization for you. Your own hairdresser or barber is a logical place for inquiries. Why not ask about the company, its products, quality of service, etc. Which products are most popular? Why? What kind of reputation does the company have? What about the competition? Customers and suppliers can also refer you to employees at the company that you could contact.

Not everyone you know is as obvious a resource as your hairdresser for a hair care products company. The remarkable thing is that you never know who is. So why not set up a big tent and invite everyone in to be part of your exploration?

PEOPLE, NOT ORGANIZATIONS, HIRE

Who needs it? People. Learning as much as possible about the individual(s) who makes hiring decisions is a key part of your research.

Who is the hiring authority?

What do you know about him?

What's important to him?

What does he look for when he hires?

What would be a "knock-out" factor for him—something that would eliminate you from consideration?

What problem could I help him solve?

Who Is the Hiring Authority?

Typically, that's the person you'll be reporting to. Depending on the kind of job you're looking for, as well as the size and type of company, there could be multiple hiring authorities for you. Executive assistants, for example, could report to many managers, any one of whom could be a hiring authority. But if you're a controller, your hiring authority would probably be the VP for finance or the president of the organization.

Determining who is the hiring authority may not be obvious. Risk managers don't always report to the VP for finance. They may be in the legal department. How can you find out? Simply call the company and ask. The receptionist may know, or you may be able to get the information from voice mail. By listening to the various options, you may not only get the name you want but learn more about how the organization is structured.

What About the Folks in Human Resources?

Most job seekers make the mistake of contacting the human resources department to inquire about jobs. The conventional wisdom is that the people in this department know about all the openings in the company. They may know about openings, but *how can they know about emerging needs of decision makers that have not yet trickled down to their department?* This happens frequently, as Charles, the industrial engineer we met in Chapter 4, learned.

Many human resources people feel they have a solemn duty to pull up the drawbridge to protect their company's executives from job seekers. Even when they're trying to fill a position, they might legitimately screen you out because of specific requirements on the job description. The decision maker, on the other hand, could be persuaded to hire you because of your compensating assets.

Example: When an additional counselor was needed for my staff, I thought that person should be at least 35 years old in order to relate well to our clients who, at that time, were all over 40. Happily, a very mature 26-year-old social worker convinced me that she was perfect for the position. She was—and became a tremendous asset to our program. But her age probably would have eliminated her from consideration if the request had been handled by a personnel department.

As an entrepreneur selling your services, be sure you're talking with someone who can buy. Doing your whole presentation with anyone else is a waste of their time. And yours!

Increasingly, companies are hedging their bets and involving several people, including those who would be your subordinates, in the selection process. Find out up front who will be involved—and when. *Simply ask: Are you the sole decision maker, or is someone else involved in making decisions of this kind?* The more you know in advance, the better you can prepare.

"Having an opportunity to learn something about the company and especially the manager of this department was probably the reason I was brought on," confides David, an account executive with LCI, International.

David knew an LCI employee from a coed softball team he had organized years before. The two met before David's interview and he "was able to get some really valuable insights about the company and the person who would be my manager. When I interviewed, we hit it off right away. We were very comfortable with each other and felt we would work well together. That proved to be the case. I have been here almost 3 years and it has been a very good experience."

KEEPING TRACK OF WHO NEEDS IT

Are You Putting This Information to Good Use?

Some job seekers get so wrapped up in research that they almost forget why they're doing it. Are you:

- ◆ feeling so comfortable in your library cocoon that you just keep amassing information?
- ◆ stuffing your pockets with scraps of paper, scribbled with unintelligible names?

Managing your information means taking control. You'll be prioritizing who needs it and organizing your data so you can use it most effectively. Good organization and follow-through can easily give you the decisive edge in getting hired.

You will be gathering information about *all* potential employers—*anyone* who could hire you. Some of these companies are, of course, much closer to your ideal than others. Keeping your goal in mind, prioritize the companies on your list into A (your ideal customer/employer), B, and C companies. Then you can organize what you have.

Getting Organized

You'll need a few simple things, like an appointments book (which lists hours of the day). Some appointments books contain a To Do list. If yours doesn't, create a central To Do list and prioritize the items (A, B, and C priorities) on your list each day. Some people are almost religious about keeping their appointments book with them at all times. Others find that too cumbersome and use an electronic message taker. One way or another, develop a systematic way to keep notes and keep your To Do list current.

You'll also need an index card file (the 4" x 6" size holds a lot of information) or PC. Each card or PC file should have the essentials: the company's name, address, phone number, type of product/service, and names of key people and their titles. If there is more than one hiring authority, make a note of that. Verify the names, spellings, pronunciation, etc., as you go along. Extra care with these details can make the difference between getting an offer and coming in second.

Each time you call, write the date and keep notes on your conversation, including such "nonessentials" as hobbies, interests, their speech patterns (impatient or slow), etc. Be sure to note anything of mutual interest. Shared enthusiasm for bass fishing, rug collecting, or your high school could be the reason you're hired. Here's an example of a file.

```
Scrubit Cleaning Service, Inc.        Tel: (555) 222-1234
22 Detergent Ave.                     Fax: (555) 222-5678
Brush Falls, OK 12345

Pres. CEO, and Hiring Auth'ty: Archibald M. Soapsuds (AMS)
V. Pres: Bea Cleaner
Treas: Sam Savett

Main Products/Services: Manufacture and distribute clean-
ing machines and equipment

3/1/95    Called for copy of annual report, other info.
3/7/95    Received info. No annual report (privately held
          co). Material included information about their
          new cleaning machines, other new products
3/10/95   Researched competitors at library. Copy of ar-
          ticle (from Cleaning Up, Feb., 1995, p. 17,
          about new cleaning machines) in file folder.
3/16/95   Misc. info (from Chamber of Commerce Leaders
          Book): AMS is member of Boy Scouts and orches-
          tra boards; enjoys golf and sailing; married.
```

Set up for follow up. How can you keep track of all the people you contact and promise to call back? Use a simple reminder system.

Tickler file—day by day. You'll need a pack of index cards and 2 sets of index card dividers. One set has the 12 months of the year; the other set has the 31 days of the month.

Let's organize the file for today: September 14. You have the month of September in front, and October, November, December, and the early months of next year following that. You'll have divider 14 in front, with 15, 16, etc., behind that. Behind your October card, you'll have days 1 through 13.

Let's say you're talking with the VP for finance at the Happy Troll Toy Co. and promise to call back the first of October. You simply make a note of your conversation on the Happy Troll card and place it in the October 1 space. At the end of the day, after you've made all the calls for September 14, you'll move card 14 to the back. With 15 facing you, you'll be ready to start your calls tomorrow.

Tickler file—hour by hour. You can also set up a tickler file for the hours of the day. That will remind you to call Jerry Waters at 2:20; Veronica Rivers at 3:00; Tracy Trickledown at 3:45; and Gary Glacier at 4:30. By making specific telephone appointments, *and calling exactly when you say you will*, you'll be making the most of your telephone time.

PLAN TO MEET ENOUGH HIRING AUTHORITIES

It Won't Happen Unless You Do

"How many appointments with decision makers have you had?" It's a question I routinely ask groups of job seekers. One or two usually volunteer: "I've had 3 appointments in 2 months." "I've had 2 appointments this month." The others are mute. Typical job seekers, like the thousands we have worked with and the respondents in our research. They hesitate, procrastinate, and wring their hands. Some blame the economy. Or Washington. And stew some more. *They simply do not meet enough people who could hire them!*

Numbers are the major barrier! And like all job-finding barriers, they're internal. You know that finding a job is a numbers game. *The more meetings you have with hiring authorities, the greater your chances of getting a job offer.* It's that simple! You can watch Pete Sampras on TV, buy the latest racket, and join a tennis club. But unless you're out on the court hitting the ball, *you're not in the game. You can't win unless you're a player!*

How many meetings with hiring authorities do you need? That depends on many factors: your experience, field, geographical area, etc. After you have been searching for a while, you may be able to develop a kind of ratio between the number of meetings with hiring authorities and job offer(s). If it took meetings with 8 hiring authorities to produce one job offer, your ratio would be 8:1.

You should also keep track of other ratios. For example, how many contacts does it take, on the average, to set up a meeting with a potential employer? That may depend on whether you're calling "cold" or using referrals. By doing both, you'll significantly speed up your job search. Let's say it takes 10 cold calls to set up a meeting with a hiring authority. Going the referral route, you find that it takes 10 calls to get 3 referrals to decision makers and that 2 of those result in appointments.

Now you have a basis for planning. You know that it will take, on the average, 10-12 calls to get a meeting with a hiring authority. And it could take meetings with 8 hiring authorities to get a job offer. Now you can set your schedule. Will you make 20 calls every day? Each week? Each month? You can estimate how long it will take to find employment. Once you develop these statistics, you can begin to predict probable outcomes. That can make a huge difference in your approach to finding employment—and in the results!

How many NOs do you need before you hear YES? The ratio may be 8:1 or 12:1. Don't get discouraged—*focus on the one!* That's an accomplishment! *The person who hears the most NOs can expect to hear the most YESs.*

It's like fishing. You know that you won't catch something each time you throw in your line. *But you know nothing will happen if you don't throw it in!*

Set up a chart to track your daily activities. (See the next page.) *Each time you call or contact a relevant person, you have accomplished something, even if the response is NO.*

If you have just started your job search, you probably have no idea what these ratios are. How do you begin?

DAILY EMPLOYER CONTACT FORM

Date_____

1. MEETINGS w/ HIRING AUTHORITIES
Name, Company   Results/Action Plan

_____
_____
_____

2. OTHER MEETINGS
Name, Company   App't date, Comments

_____
_____
_____
_____

3. TELEPHONE CONTACTS
Name, Company   Results/Action Plan

_____
_____
_____
_____
_____
_____

4. LETTERS SENT
Name, Company   Purpose/Plan

_____
_____
_____
_____

5. RESEARCH
Name, Company

_____
_____
_____
_____

Overplan. More is better. Overplan your day because inevitably, there'll be last minute changes and cancellations. If you've overplanned, you'll have constructive things to do and won't waste your precious time.[3]

MANAGE TO MEET ENOUGH HIRING AUTHORITIES

Value Your Time

Your time is every bit as precious as when you were employed. But using it wisely is more difficult. "Unstructured time, the lack of a schedule" is one of the most unsettling aspects of unemployment, our survey respondents indicated.

Finding a job is a full-time job, 40 hours a week. It means getting up each morning, dressing for work, and going to work in your office. Whether it's at home or an outplacement office, the important thing is that you are working. Your DO NOT DISTURB sign is on the door. *Treat your time exactly as if you were employed. You must be even more disciplined!*

Plan to Make Your Time Count [4]

9:00–9:15	Start your day with something positive. Do something you enjoy.
9:15–12:00	Calls to relevant people.

- ◆ Talk with at least 10 relevant persons, including hiring authorities.
- ◆ Set up at least 1 appointment with a hiring authority that week.
- ◆ Set up at least 1 appointment with a relevant person for that week.

12:00–1:00	Lunch
1:00–2:30	Travel and appointment
2:30–3:30	Library research on additional companies
3:45–4:30	Correspondence, including thank-you notes to people you've met
4:30–5:00	Plan for next day/week

- ◆ List tasks you must accomplish on your To Do list, including specific people you will call.
- ◆ Prioritize your tasks (A, B, C)

5:00–5:15	Reward time

Reward Yourself!

Check off each call as you go through your list and set up appointments. Then *reward yourself! Celebrate each achievement each day!* Treat yourself to something nice—something you will enjoy. Whether it is a cup of tea, a walk in the park, a call to a friend—it's important to give yourself the recognition that you have accomplished something valuable that day. Having something to celebrate each day will help you maintain a positive attitude—your essential partner.

Don't Get Overwhelmed!

Professional recruiters can make 50 calls in a 2 1/2-hour period, but we know that few job seekers can do even half that many. One Sale to Success graduate developed what he called "A Shy Person's Guide to Finding Employment."

"Thirty calls a day is overwhelming to people like me. But 10 calls a day is not. I decided that I could push myself that hard. So that's the goal I set. And I really committed myself to doing it every day.

"I also make one appointment each day to meet with someone. Anyone. A networking contact or someone else. The appointment gets you out of the house and gets the juices flowing. Eventually, I met with someone who was impressed with my experience and hired me!"

By adding one meeting with a hiring authority each week, you'll shorten your job search significantly.

Our Shy Persons' Guide to Employment

Make a commitment to:

- ◆ contact at least 10 relevant persons each day, preferably by phone.
- ◆ meet at least one relevant person each day, and
- ◆ meet at least one hiring authority each week.

Although that's a very modest commitment for full-time job seekers, it's more than most of our survey respondents report. Only 3% indicate that they network daily with 10 or more people. Seventy-two percent network daily with 3 or fewer.

Circulate. Moving around is not only good for your heart, it's good for your spirits. Make it your business to get out of the house. Do things with your family, friends, and other people—volunteer work, for example.

Keep Score

How do you eat an elephant?[5] One bite at a time! Monitoring your progress is essential. At the end of each day, take half an hour to review your Employer Contact Forms. Measure your results against your plan.

How many calls did you make?

How many appointments with hiring authorities?

How many other relevant appointments did you set?

Did you get any offers?

What did you learn?

What can you do better?

How can you waste less time?

Review your activity. After 21 days, review your activity and measure your progress.[6] Are you making enough calls? Are you seeing enough hiring authorities? Some people work well in a pattern of intensive activity and a break. If you've made dozens of calls and seen 10 decision makers, you deserve a nice, long weekend. Other people prefer the slower, steadier approach. It doesn't matter whether you're a turtle or a hare. Just be sure you have enough activity going so you'll reach your destination.

If you cannot meet your goal, don't sweat it. Reset it! Revise your 6-month goal. If you have accomplished only half of it, you're still way ahead of all those people who have set no goals at all.[7]

One way to take a positive look at what you've accomplished is to use a cumulative graph rather than sheer numbers. If your objective is to make

10 calls each day and you make only 7 on one day, 9 on another and 3 on another, you'll see yourself falling short and you're apt to be disheartened. By putting the same figures on a cumulative graph, however, though it's still apparent that you haven't met your goal, you can see that you have accomplished a lot. You'll feel better about yourself and what you have achieved.[8]

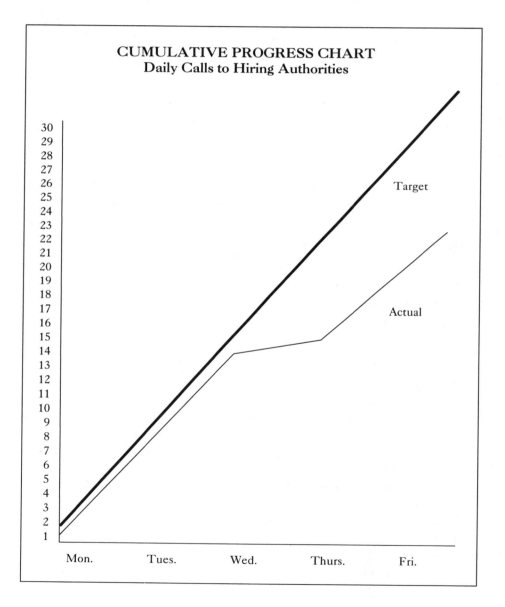

CUMULATIVE PROGRESS CHART
Daily Calls to Hiring Authorities

MANAGE YOUR TIME WHEN YOU'RE EMPLOYED

Job hunting while you're employed is both a blessing and a curse. The good news is that you're more employable when you're employed. From the employer's perspective, you're more desirable. And you're probably feeling more confident and better about yourself than if you were unemployed.

Take advantage of the many resources you have as an employee. That does not mean the photocopier and fax machine. But as an employee, you are usually in a much better position to change jobs because you're in contact with many people who could help you.

Some questions you might ask yourself:

1. Are there opportunities right here in my organization?
2. Are there people I interact with (clients, customers, suppliers) who can help me learn about opportunities outside my organization?
3. Are there professionals who can help me make a job or career change?

1. There might be an excellent opportunity right down the hall—or on the next floor. Why not put on your Sherlock Holmes hat and find out more about your organization? Depending on the size and type of company, you could learn a lot by getting to know people in other departments. If you're in the retail department at your bank, get acquainted with some of the folks in the trust department. And advertising. Who are they? What do they do? Does it sound interesting? How is their work changing? What skills do they value? Are they skills you have? What would it take for you to acquire them?

There may be no "opening" right now, but what about the future? Because you're enterprising, you're looking beyond the immediate situation and exploring ways you might be helpful to them. As an employee, you have a great advantage because most companies prefer to hire from within.

Internal networking is easy and accessible, yet most people tend to limit themselves to the group they work with. That's unfortunate, because your next job could be much closer than you think. That was Norman's experience. A researcher in organic chemistry, he was about to relocate to another state for a job he was not particularly happy about. Fortunately, before he accepted that position, he discovered a more interesting opportunity in a lab right down the hall.

2. The people you do business with are another terrific resource. Laura, a 42-year-old dental hygienist, decided that she didn't want to spend the rest of her life cleaning other people's teeth. Although she wasn't sure what she wanted, she was intrigued by the idea of being a pharmaceutical rep. "But I really don't know much about what they do," she confessed, "or if I could get that kind of job."

Laura's best resources—representatives from many major pharmaceutical houses—came into her office frequently to see her boss and her. Laura's second job now is to begin learning about the industry and what pharmaceutical reps do. By contacting the reps she knows on her day off, Laura can learn about their jobs and can get the inside story about their companies.

Laura also has a chance to judge the products and the way they're sold. She can ask her boss—as well as other dentists—which products and presentations they like. And why. After a trip to the library, she can pull all that information together before she contacts the companies.

3. Recruiters and career management consultants are professionals who may be able to help you. As an employed person, you may want to develop a relationship with a recruiter who specializes in your field and works with people at your level of experience. If you're an upper-level executive, a retainer search firm may be appropriate. These recruiters are paid by corporations on a retainer basis to locate top executives for specific positions.

Contingency search firms are another type of recruiter. As the name suggests, they are paid by the company seeking a new employee only when the recruiter's candidate is hired. Contingency search firms usually place people in mid-level positions, although there is some overlap with retainer firms.

To have a good working relationship with a recruiter, you'll want to do more than mail your resume. Meet that person, be sure you are comfortable with them and that they understand your job needs.

Time Management Is Essential

There is, of course, the downside to finding another job while you're working. Obviously, it's a squeeze to find time to call, do research, and meet people. That makes planning even more important. You have no time to waste. Take full advantage of the hours before and after work, as well as lunchtime. Then, of course, there are vacation days, which no one likes to sacrifice. But once you decide what's important, you'll use your time accordingly.

EMPLOYMENT INSURANCE CHECKLIST

✓ Who needs what you're selling?

✓ Can you describe your ideal customer?

✓ How many are there?

✓ Who else would buy your services?

✓ Do you have a list of potential customers?

✓ Did you prioritize the list (A, B, and C customers)?

✓ Did you research these companies?

✓ Are you talking with knowledgeable people?

✓ Is your information well organized?

✓ Do you have a tickler file?

✓ Do you plan each day to use your time well?

✓ Are you making at least 10 calls each day?

✓ Are you meeting at least one hiring authority each week?

✓ Are you monitoring your progress against your plan?

✓ If you're employed, are you using the many resources that can help you find another job?

CHAPTER 7

❖

Networking:
Making Connections

How Can You Contact Hiring Authorities?

"**Network!** That's what everyone told me," the former hospital administrator exclaimed. "But I didn't know what that meant or what I was supposed to do!"

Erica was neither naive nor lacking in social skills. Quite the contrary. Her consensus-building abilities were so superior that she had been repeatedly reelected chairperson of a major policy-making committee for the large institution where she had worked.

"The people at the outplacement company told me to call my friends. Find out if there are any jobs. That didn't sound right to me. So I called my friends and asked about their children."

Networking. It's a term so widely used that most people won't admit that they don't know what it is. Or how to do it.

What's a Network?

It is simply people you know and the people they can link you to. Even if you're not particularly gregarious or well connected, you know hundreds of people. All your friends, acquaintances, relatives, neighbors, business associates, members of your church or synagogue, people you know through alumni and civic organizations, your doctor and dentist—*everyone* you know. Because these people can connect you to hundreds, even thousands of other people, your potential network is vast.

TRADITIONAL NETWORKING

Asking for Help

You have probably been urged, like Erica, to contact everyone you know and ask them to help you. The conventional advice: *Get "information interviews."* This amounts to saying to your network contact, *"I want you to give me your time—maybe just 20 or 30 minutes.* What's in it for you, Ms. Contact? Nothing! But you can relax. I'm following traditional networking rules. *I won't ask you for a job!"*

So you proceed to network.

1. You talk with your friend A.
2. You explain that you are looking for a job and ask if she knows about any openings in your field.
3. A suggests you talk with B, who "may have an opening or may know someone who does."
4. You contact B, explaining that A (your *bridge*) suggested that you call.
5. B explains that he has no openings but suggests that you call C.
6. Because B doesn't know you, he cannot honestly recommend you.
7. You may be feeling uncomfortable because you don't know B or C. When C's secretary informs you that C is at a meeting and C doesn't return your calls, you find it difficult to be persistent. You don't want to "bother" him and seem too "pushy," so you probably give up.

Problems with Traditional Networking

Traditional networking is based on the assumption that people will take the time to assist you—*and every other job seeker who asks*. While most people are cooperative and helpful, they are also busy and increasingly under the gun to be productive. How your network contact responds to your request for "20 or 30 minutes" probably depends on his relationship to the referring person, time constraints, etc. He will be asking himself: *How important (to him) is the referring individual?*

Let's imagine that there is a continuum of power and influence for that particular businessperson. Everyone in *his* network falls somewhere on that continuum. If the referring person (your bridge) is his most important customer, his favorite uncle, or the governor, the businessperson will probably "make" time to help you.

But if the bridge is only a casual acquaintance, he's apt to be "too busy right now." *His busy schedule may legitimately preclude even a brief meeting if there seems to be no compelling reason to see you.*

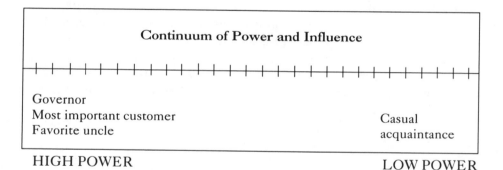

Put on his socks for a moment. What is he thinking? *The job seeker said that he would* not *ask me for a job: He just wants "some information."* (That is supposed to be reassuring, but it could be insulting, or at least off-putting.) *Apparently, he has no particular interest in this company as a place to work. Why doesn't he want a job here? Aren't we good enough for him?* The network contact would be justified in concluding: *This job seeker cannot benefit me or my company. So why should I take the time to talk with him?*

How easy for him to say: "I'm sorry. We don't have any openings right now. Why don't you send me your resume?" And he is off the hook—literally.

Asking for names of people you could talk with is an easier request to fulfill. But your network contact has only a limited amount of "good will" or political capital with each of *her* business friends. If she's smart, she'll use it sparingly. Each time she suggests the name of someone you might contact, she's spending some of that limited resource. She's already giving you some of her time. Why should she also spend her political capital for you?

Why People Don't Network

Many job seekers, like Erica, who have extensive networks, don't use them to find jobs because:

- They feel as though they are *using* others.
- They are acknowledging their need for assistance (often an excruciating experience for people who are accustomed to being in control).

"It's the first time in my life that I feel a total loss of control," she lamented. "I was always the strong one. I never needed help. I need to help others." Like so many competent people who were "doing everything right," she felt deeply humiliated by her job loss. By asking for help (some go so far as to call it "begging"), they feel they are announcing their "failure" to the world.

For both parties, traditional networking is often inadequate. The networker dislikes asking for help and is bothered by the idea of *using* the other person. The network contact, on the other hand, may have little incentive to *make* time to fulfill the request.

ANOTHER APPROACH TO NETWORKING

Offer to Help

Networking can be a win-win experience when it's *mutually beneficial, shared* assistance and information. By using this approach, you can reinforce your network, rather than draw from it.

Instead of asking *for* help, offer *to* help!

What a difference a preposition can make! It signals a 180-degree change in perspective. Now you are "them" oriented, rather than "me" oriented. *By asking: "What can I do for you," rather than "What can you do for me," you'll probably get more information and you:*

- *are more likely to accomplish your first objective*—a face-to-face meeting.

- *strengthen your own position and confidence.* By offering to assist, rather than asking for help, you put yourself on an equal footing with the contact.
- *recognize that he's interested in what's in it for him.* Show that you have something of value to offer (yourself and your services).
- *focus your attention on the contact and his needs,* demonstrating your interest in that person and the organization.
- *can determine whether or not there is some task or activity you could do.*
- *expand your network.*

From the network contact's point of view, this approach is surely preferable. He's probably thinking:

- *This job seeker is appealing to my self-interest* (as well as my company's needs).
- *He's talking about my problems, not his.*
- By asking intelligent questions about our company and listening to my answers, *he certainly seemed interested in what we do here.*
- *He's made a good impression* simply doing that.
- Even though we're not sure how he could help us, I probably should meet with him. *He may have some ideas on how we could move ahead on our dandelion distribution project—our top priority.*
- We don't need anyone full-time, but we do have that orangutan feeding problem that's been so difficult. *Maybe he has some ideas about solving that.*
- I'm encouraging him to stay in touch. *You never know when we could use someone like that around here.*

It's during these exchanges, when people can discuss their needs, that mutually beneficial opportunities may develop.

Make EVERY Meeting an Information Interview

Become an Info Sponge. That's not a mysterious creature of the deep. It's you—in your Sherlock Holmes hat, with your ever-ready notepad in your pocket. Why limit yourself to information interviews when you can learn a lot more informally? *Every* conversation you have—with neighbors, relatives, friends, colleagues—is a chance to learn something. Or it's a lost opportunity. Every social situation, from neighborhood block parties to class reunions to holiday parties, is an excellent time to get "caught up" on what's going on in other people's companies. You're asking questions about business, industry, new developments, specific companies, who works there, their competition, the decision makers, etc.

FROM NETWORKING TO SAFETY NET(WORK)

The Need

We all rely on others for friendship, support, information, and our need to feel connected to a community: our safety net(work). The relationships you build become your interpersonal security system. Support systems have always been important. Nowadays, they're more vital than ever because of:

- ◆ changes in families and communities, including
  - ◆ mobility (physical separation) and
  - ◆ social disintegration of families
- ◆ changes in the workplace, including
  - ◆ shorter duration of jobs
  - ◆ less job security
  - ◆ more contract, temporary, and part-time work
  - ◆ more people working at home, isolated from others

Having a good support system in place when you're unemployed can make a huge difference in how well you fare—and how long you're unemployed. Let's face it. Being unemployed is no picnic. You need all the support you can get. The network you have developed over the years will not only help keep you afloat, it's your best source of information. You'll recall that *inadequate* information is what separates you from your next employer. So whether you're employed or not, the care and feeding of your network should be a top priority.

One of the hazards of being "married to your job" is that when it ends, some key relationships may also end. Many outplaced executives learned that painful lesson.

"I'll never again devote so much of myself to my job that I neglect other vital relationships like business contacts and family . . . Don't neglect your network . . . Keep your network active."

Three additional facts should be remembered:

1. The average young worker will have at least 10 jobs in his or her career.
2. Most people (60—70%) find employment through someone they know.
3. Your network will shrink unless you reinvigorate and expand it. That's because, inevitably, some people in your network move away, die, or disappear from view. So you have to keep fostering good relationships and reaching out to new people just to sustain your network.

How Do You Reinforce Your Safety Net(work)?

1. Think of yourself as a resource. A particularly good time to be supportive of others is when you are employed. *Before* you need help. But every day is a good day to do something for someone. Investing in others is nourishing your safety net, as well as theirs, because it makes you both feel good. Do it because you want to, not because you expect anything in return.

2. Listen. Most people love to talk about themselves. By listening, you'll create fertile soil for relationships to blossom. Good listeners are also rewarded with more accurate information, a better understanding of oneself and others, and much more.

You can improve your listening habits if you want to. Start by listening to yourself. Becoming aware of your listening habits is the first step to improving them. Ask yourself these questions:

- ◆ Do you usually talk more than you listen?
- ◆ What are your listening strengths?
- ◆ What are your weaknesses?
- ◆ Do you frequently interrupt?
- ◆ Do you daydream?
- ◆ Do you jump to conclusions?

Some specific suggestions to enhance your listening skills:

- ◆ **Choose to listen.** We've been given two ears and one mouth, perhaps so that we can listen twice as much as we talk.
- ◆ **Be attentive physically as well as mentally.** Face the person, make eye contact, and relax.
- ◆ **Block out distractions** and competing thoughts. Avoid "rehearsing" your response while the speaker is talking.
- ◆ **Encourage the speaker** with "I'm listening" responses such as nodding your head and "Uh,huh . . . I see . . . Interesting!"
- ◆ **Focus on the speaker:**
  - ◆ *what* is being said, and
  - ◆ *how* it is being said: the tone and body language.
- ◆ **Keep an open mind,** showing respect. Avoid judging too soon and being preoccupied with the speaker's mannerisms.
- ◆ **Acknowledge the speaker's feelings. Empathize.**
- ◆ **Clarify by asking questions.** Don't assume you understand what the speaker's words mean to the speaker.
- ◆ **Keep your emotions in check.** If the speaker becomes emotional or uses emotional words, avoid overreacting.
- ◆ **Paraphrase** ("What I hear you saying is . . . In other words, you think that . . .") and *summarize* to be sure you understand what the speaker is saying from his or her point of view.
- ◆ **Finally, there is no magic formula.** If you want to be a better listener, you will be!

3. Respond and connect with the speaker's interests. What mutual interests do you have? Smiling, nodding, and asking questions are fine, but not enough. Let them know enough about you so they'll see you as knowledgeable, intelligent, "up" on what's going on in your field. You can gain credibility by mentioning an accomplishment, people you've worked with, etc. Fact dropping, as well as name dropping, can communicate that you're "in the know."

- ◆ Have you heard about the merger between Peptic Pork Rinds and No Win Noodles? Do you think they'll be laying off people?

- ◆ Did you read the article in today's paper about the president of Incontinent Investments retiring? Do you think there'll be a big shake-up in the company?

- ◆ I did some strategic planning for Misguided Moving and Storage and Manny Misguided was so pleased with my work that he has recommended me to Mismatched Furniture. Do you know anyone at Mismatched?

Your mutual interest isn't necessarily work related, of course. It can be anything—the NBA, the PTA, or the AARP. You're more likely to develop a business friendship if you offer to help in some way, like sending him a copy of the article you discussed. Or calling back with an address of an organization she wanted. By listening, bonding, finding a mutual interest and offering to help, you'll develop more business friends, broaden your horizons, and invigorate your safety net(work). And you'll enjoy doing it!

YOUR SAFETY NET(WORK)

Different Kinds of Threads

The composition of your network isn't uniform. Some threads are longer and stronger than others. Many of those people will want to help you because they like you. You're a friend. And you've helped them in the past. Or you're family. (They may like you anyway.)

Some people you know seem to like you. You just "hit it off" right away. There's some chemistry between you and that's a real plus. Obviously, the more people who like you, the better.

Others in your network—possibly some of the key people—may not be your best buddies. But they know what you're capable of doing. And they respect you. It's great to be well liked. But it's essential to be respected. Respect is the crucial element—the medium of exchange—in business relationships.

Who Are the Key People in Your Network?

They're probably people who like *and* respect you—people you trust to listen, understand, and make good suggestions. They could be anyone—your spouse, aunt, former boss, lawyer, or school friend.

Business friends[1] are probably your best link to your next job because they know you, know what you can do, and respect you. They're people you've done business with—your clients, customers, and colleagues, as well as people you've worked with in the community.

Your business friends know that you're a terrific graphics person who did a sensational job on the company's promotional material. Or that you're a crackerjack lab technician who could always be counted on to get accurate results. It's a business friend who knows that you're the kind of person who does what it takes to make things right for the customer. Like going to his warehouse at 8:00 p.m. to inspect the damaged delivery and replace it even though it meant working two 12-hour days. These people have confidence that you'll do a good job and follow through. So they can recommend you. They may even contact you if they hear about an opportunity.

How Can You Expand Your Network?

- **Start with your most trusted advisers** and ask them for names of people you could talk with. You should be able to get at least three names from each of them.

- **Trade and professional associations** can be outstanding resources. The Yellow Pages of your phone book list many of them under "Associations." If you want to explore further, look into the Encyclopedia of Associations[2] at your library. The scope and variety of the 22,000-plus organizations described in this three-volume set are awesome. For example, there's an Electronic Funds Transfer Association, based in Herndon, Virginia. If you're a pheasant fancier, you can join the World Pheasant Association of the U.S.A., headquartered in Hacienda Heights, California. And would you believe that there's a National Orientation Directors Association, based in Knoxville, Tennessee, for college and university personnel who deal with orientation programs for their students?

- Meetings of groups of people whose interests you share are, clearly, ideal networking opportunities. If you haven't been active in a group with a particular focus, why not get involved now? You could, for example, offer to help with membership. Or a special project. You'll be contacting and working with people with whom you have something important in common.

- **High school and college alumni groups are terrific networks.** Because you're part of the "family," fellow alumni want you to succeed. Remarkably, even recent grads often overlook the tremendous potential of alumni and alumni organizations. Most colleges and universities offer assistance to job seekers, and many have networking groups to facilitate the process.

- **Be inclusive.** Draw everyone you know and everyone you meet into your network. Starting with your holiday card list, you can probably come up with about 200 names. If you can't, sit down with your family and friends. Brainstorm!

- **Don't overlook your doctor, dentist, neighborhood shopkeepers,** and others that you interact with. One client, for example, was referred to the president of a prestigious advertising agency by a local art gallery. When he brought in a picture for repair, this client mentioned that he was looking for a position using his creative writing skills.

"Why don't you call CV, of CV Advertising?" they suggested. "He's one of our best clients. Of course you may use our name."

◆ **"It's not what you know . . . "** The familiar message: powerful people can help you. In fact, *anyone with information can help you.* And that's almost everyone. They're not necessarily the chief honchos, the visible, well-known executives who are apt to be "networked out." Others in the organization may be just as knowledgeable, and even more helpful because they're flattered that you asked for their advice.

◆ **Reach out.** Strangers are friends you haven't met yet. You can change that by initiating a conversation. I had a delightful experience doing that with a couple who had adjacent seats at a concert series. When the man commented knowledgeably and enthusiastically after a violin concerto, I asked if he was a musician.

"No, I was the head of BW's business school for 17 years," he explained, "and after I retired, I was asked to be a vice president with XYZ" (an international outplacement firm). We enjoyed a nice chat, exchanged business cards, and ultimately arranged for me to do some work for XYZ.

Serendipity happens. Another example involved an accountant, a native of Kenya, who was job hunting in a suburban Cleveland office complex. Hearing a woman with a distinctive accent nearby, he asked where she was from.

When she replied "South Africa," an animated conversation ensued, during which the accountant mentioned that he had just interviewed for a job. The woman mentioned that her husband was vice president for finance for a very successful retail apparel chain headquartered nearby.

"I know they haven't done their bank reconciliation for 12 months. Should I call him to see if he would like to meet you?" the woman asked. He did. And for the next 10 years, the accountant from Kenya helped her husband's company expand to 160 stores.

◆ **Volunteer.** It's a great way to meet people, feel good about yourself, learn a new skill, and explore new kinds of organizations. It can be an excellent investment and a very positive experience. But *don't simply give away your time!* That could leave you feeling abused. One young woman, for example, complained bitterly because she still had no job after providing public relations work for a city administration for 3 years! Clearly, she had *allowed* herself to be taken advantage of.

To avoid that, be clear about what you're offering to do. Working on a specific project or event could be a rewarding experience, like contacting 10 companies for United Way contributions. Or selling advertising space in the program book for an upcoming charity event. Set specific limits regarding what you'll do and your time frame. You might want to volunteer for one week, one day a week for a month or two, etc. Don't allow your volunteering to be so open-ended that you risk becoming a full-time volunteer!

Volunteering to write articles, give talks, or moderate panel discussions is an excellent way to gain visibility and credibility in your field. For example, when Jessica offered to moderate a panel discussion at the NW Regional Conference of Dandelion Growers of America, she not only gained recognition, she saved the $350 conference registration fee.

◆ **Make lemonade when life gives you lemons.** You can make your network blossom simply by thinking positively. Transform an unsuccessful, even painful experience like being turned down for a job into something good by making a new friend. (See Chapter 16.)

No Safety Net?

If you're young, inexperienced, or new to town, you may think you're at a big disadvantage. No business friends. No mentors. But look at the positives. Everyone loves to give advice—especially to young people. All you have to do is listen. You'll make the seniors feel great—and you can start your network.

Being new to town may be even better because most residents are quite gracious to newcomers. Jill found that she could get in to see virtually anyone she called when she explained that she was a clinical data analyst and said: "I'm new in town. We just moved here from Boston and I've heard that you are the best person to talk with about . . ."

You can only sell what you honestly have. If it's being new in town, sell that! Start with the few people you do know—even if it's only the three guys on the moving truck and your next-door neighbor. They each know another three or four people. Before long, you'll have a real network. Build on what you have, even if it's just a thread. Spiders do it all the time!

NETWORKING TIPS

Some Tips for Large Group Situations

Networking can be a mutually beneficial experience if you are interested in others, bond with them, and help them whenever you can. Here are some suggestions:

1. Come prepared with:
   - some business cards which are readily available so you'll avoid fumbling
   - your brief "sound bite" explaining who you are, what you do. For example:

   Hi! I'm Lila Lee. I've been doing market development for Leaping Lizards Dance Company. Have you ever seen any of our performances? (Wait for answer.) I see, you don't care for modern dance. You prefer jazz. What kind of jazz do you like best, Larry?

   Hi! I'm Jesse James and I developed the first guided tour program for Jurassic Park. Have you ever gone on one of our tours? (Wait for answer.) Oh, that's too bad. I see from your name tag that you're with Multiple Fruitflies. What kind of work do you do there, Jane?

   Hi! I'm Benny Banana and I've been doing quality control for Idle Idols. We did such a good job of streamlining production that only one junior person handles all the quality control now. I see you're with Instant Icons. How long have you been with the company, Ivan?

2. Have a clear objective: What do you want to accomplish at this gathering? For example, you're interested in international trade and want to learn more about two of the heavy hitters: Muddle-Through International and Worldwide Whirligigs.
3. Arrive early so you can circulate.
4. Introduce yourself to others with a smile and firm handshake.
5. Ask questions, maintaining eye contact.
6. Listen attentively to what the other person says.
7. Connect with them on a mutual interest.
8. Collect business cards that you can follow up on later, but remember that your objective is not amassing cards.
9. Follow up. After the meeting:
   - Make notes on the business cards re: date, place, information about the person.

- ◆ Call and set up meetings.
- ◆ Send a thank-you note if someone has been helpful.

Shy Persons' Guide to Networking

If the thought of talking with new people gives you palpitations, set a more modest goal. Initiate a conversation with one person. Start by making eye contact, introducing yourself with a smile and handshake. If name tags are used, they provide an obvious opening.

- ◆ Is their name unusual?
- ◆ Do you know someone who is (might be) related?
- ◆ If the company is identified, you could ask about it, the industry, etc.

Name tag or not, you can always ask:

- ◆ What do you do?
- ◆ How long have you been doing it?
- ◆ How did you get into this kind of work?
- ◆ What do you like about it?
- ◆ Any negatives?
- ◆ What school did you go to? Etc.

If you're genuinely interested in others, you won't seem too pushy. The keys are listening and developing some common bond. Networking is not only fun. It's a marvelous way to gather information, especially about *who needs it* and *how you can reach them*. Be sure you're asking questions in a pleasant, conversational way so it doesn't seem like an interrogation.

You may also meet decision makers through networking, but that usually requires other methods, as we'll see in the next several chapters.

EMPLOYMENT INSURANCE CHECKLIST

- ✓ Do you have a list of everyone in your network?
- ✓ Do you think of yourself as a resource?
- ✓ Do you offer to help whenever possible?
- ✓ Do you make every meeting an "information interview"?
- ✓ Are you listening actively?
- ✓ Do you focus on the other person and their needs?
- ✓ Do you have business friends who can recommend you?
- ✓ Do people know what you have done and are capable of doing?
- ✓ Are you continuing to expand and strengthen your network?

CHAPTER 8

❖

The Paper Chase
Part 1: Resumes

BEYOND NETWORKING

If job seekers have a favorite sport, it's networking. It's an excellent way to learn about employers, the industry, specific companies, and hiring authorities. Knowledgeable people can help you answer the second and third questions in your marketing plan: who needs it (your services)? and how can you reach them? Networking is, clearly, a powerful vehicle, but there are other ways to meet and persuade decision makers. Why not use them all?

RESUME MYTHS AND REALITIES

Will Resumes Get You the Job?

For most job seekers, communicating with prospective employers means resumes because it is widely assumed that resumes get jobs. That's more myth than reality, according to some experts. Richard Nelson Bolles, author of *What Color Is Your Parachute?*, for example, begins his discussion about resumes with the heading: "Our Favorite Way of Avoiding Rejection: Resumes." He continues, "Resumes have a lousy track record. A study of employers done a number of years ago discovered that there was one job offer, tendered and accepted, for every 1,470 resumes that employers received from job hunters."[1]

Resumes are rarely the "door openers" that their proponents claim. In fact, they are more likely to screen you *out* than *in*. Why? Because companies receive resumes by the truckload, they use almost any excuse to get rid of them:

- ◆ you have too much experience—or not enough;
- ◆ your experience is too limited—or not specific enough;

- ◆ you worked only for major companies—don't understand small company mentality;
- ◆ you have done only operations—we want an operations/marketing person;
- ◆ you have no degree—or have too many degrees;
- ◆ you changed jobs too often—or stayed in same job too long;
- ◆ you worked for Global Chemicals (too expensive for us)
- ◆ you graduated from Harvard (I went to State U.)
- ◆ all your experience is in health care; this job is in retail;
- ◆ you managed a large group—won't be satisfied with a smaller staff;
- ◆ you did only military research—won't understand industrial needs etc., etc., etc.

Resumes are, after all, only pieces of paper. They have no smile, energy, or depth. There's no "chemistry." No warm handshake.[2] Even the best resume doesn't tell prospective employers what they want to know: *What can you do for us now and in the future?* It can only highlight what you *have done.* You may be just what they need—but can they tell that from your resume?

Five Experts: Six Opinions

There's no consensus about the effectiveness of resumes, how and when they should be used, which format is best, etc. If you ask five resume "experts," you're apt to get six opinions. Or more! Despite all that, you'll be expected to have a resume. If you are revising yours or starting out fresh, here are some things to consider.

TEN RESUME BASICS

1. It's a marketing tool. Your resume is an integral part of your marketing plan and can help reinforce the positive impression you make. It confirms your statements about your work history, responsibilities, accomplishments (which you should quantify whenever possible), education, etc. You're presenting accurate information about yourself in an interesting, favorable way, explaining what you're selling and why prospective employers should hire you.

Like all tools, your resume will "work" only in appropriate situations. You don't market in a vacuum. Your resume must be

- ◆ directed to the right people and
- ◆ potentially valuable to them.

Getting your resume in the hands of a decision maker is not enough. It must get their attention and generate a sufficiently positive response that they will want to act on your behalf.

Marketing yourself and using your resume as a marketing tool means making the most of what you honestly have to offer. Just as your mini-stories emphasize your accomplishments, you'll be describing yourself in active terms, communicating that you're a results-oriented person who can benefit your next employer.

That's standard resume advice. Unfortunately, not everyone reads books like this. Or acts on what they read. If they did, there would be no resumes from American-born college graduates which begin like this (and continue in a similar fashion):

FOREIGN LANGUAGE

- ◆ Able to read, write, speak, instruct, translate, and interpret in Spanish.
- ◆ Assisted in teaching English to speakers of other languages.

This person has impressive language skills, but his resume, beginning with the inert "able to read," is woefully weak. Simply turning these sentences around, starting with action verbs, improves them.

FOREIGN LANGUAGE SKILLS

- Instructed, translated, and interpreted in Spanish, orally and in writing
- Taught English as a second language, assisting instructor

Additional accurate information could, of course, significantly strengthen these statements. For example:

FOREIGN LANGUAGE SKILLS

- Instructed _____ students in Spanish, ____ of whom continued with the next course in Spanish, a _____ % increase from previous year.
- Translated ____ articles from Spanish to English.
  - Complimented by author(s) for skillful translations.
  - Completed all assignments on time.
- Interpreted for ____ Spanish-speaking clients who needed assistance in communicating with the public school system.

---

2. Preparing your resume is valuable. Many job seekers plunge into resume writing prematurely, before they've really thought about what they're looking for and where they might go. That's like starting out on a long journey without money, a map, or a toothbrush. Happily, you've done all your preliminary work already. You've assessed yourself, written your goal, analyzed your accomplishments, and learned to look at yourself from the employer's perspective. You have thought about your values and what gives you satisfaction, as well as what you want to do and the kind of environment that suits you best. All of that vital information is on your worksheets, your Goal Setting/Planning Guide, and your mini-story guide.

Having done that, writing your resume should be relatively easy. It's the end product of all your soul-searching, a place to highlight facts about you, your achievements, and how you have benefited your employers. Be sure your accomplishments get the attention they deserve. Your resume is no place for buried treasures.

3. What's in and what's out? Obviously, you cannot bare all on one or two pages. You must be selective. And there are some rather standard guidelines to help you determine what to include, such as:

- ◆ name, address, telephone number(s)
- ◆ job objective and/or summary highlighting your major qualifications
- ◆ responsibilities (employment history)
- ◆ accomplishments and skills
- ◆ education, including degrees, institution, major fields of study. If your minor could make a major difference, include that. Also include continuing education, which demonstrates that you're always learning and growing—the kind of person they want to hire.
- ◆ awards, recognition, certificates, etc.
- ◆ professional/trade/industry associations

What's out? Omit data, like your height and weight, the names and ages of your children, your marital status, and other information that is not job-related, as well as salary and references.

An exception might be community activities, especially if you have had major responsibilities in noncontroversial organizations. If, for example, you're on the board of a hospital, conduct a volunteer orchestra, or serve as treasurer of your condominium association, you're providing evidence of your leadership capabilities. For young people without much work experience, some impressive extra-curricular activities, especially if they complement a good GPA, could give you a competitive edge.

4. It should look good. One page or two? That really depends on how much the recipient(s) should know about you. One page may be preferable, but not if it means a resume that requires a shoehorn. Resumes with tiny type and 1/4-inch margins punish both the reader and the sender. Spreading the same information on two pages can transform it into a marketing tool for you.

Clearly, your resume should look good and be easy to read at a glance (20 to 30 seconds), since that's all the time most people will give to it. Another bit of common sense about which there should be no debate: no errors. No spelling errors. No punctuation errors. No grammatical errors. Not even one.

5. The head should fit the body. If you state a job objective at the top, be sure it's supported by the body—the facts about you, your accomplishments, and the benefits you can bring to the company. That's often a real challenge for career changers, who may find that their resumes hurt more than they help.

That was Doug's situation. A skilled purchasing manager, he pointed out in his resume that he had saved his employer many thousands of dollars during his 23 years with LTV Steel. But technology had dramatically reduced job opportunities for steel purchasers. The energetic 48-year old wanted to try "the other side of the desk—sales." Having worked with salespeople throughout his career, Doug was sure he could do a good job of persuading others.

But his resume gave no hint that he could sell! Following my suggestion that he forget about his resume, talk with some sales managers, and explain what he could do for them, he was hired within a few weeks and has been happily selling new cars ever since.

6. Don't let it victimize you. Some job hunters allow their resumes to lash them to the past just as firmly as Gulliver was tied down by the Lilliputians. That happens often, not only to career changers like Doug but to people like Steve. His job as vice president for communications of a mid-sized corporation ended almost four years ago. Since then, he has mailed hundreds of resumes all over the country. But no job has surfaced. Frustrated, Steve blames his former title. "I wish I never had that title: vice president. People see that and think they can't afford me. In fact, all I had was the title. No staff."

The solution? Some people would advise omitting the title altogether. Overlooking facts that might be threatening, like advanced degrees, is not unusual, but leaving out the title of your position on a resume is a glaring omission. Could he change the title to something less intimidating? Yes, conceivably, if he could discuss the change with his former employer. But that would not be totally honest, and even if someone at the company agreed, the discrepancy could be noticed and boomerang. Prospective employers are, understandably, very wary about anything that smacks of dishonesty.

Steve's best strategy is to avoid sending out his resume and use other means to contact hiring authorities. When he meets them, he could explain away this trivial item (if it comes up) and they could focus on what's important: what he could do for them.

7. Become a custom tailor. You know what you are selling. Who needs it? Who will be reading your resume? Why? What are they looking for? Before you write your resume, research the company, the position (if there is one), and the hiring authority. A one-size-fits-all resume is really a "shot in the dark." Why shoot in the dark when you can bring in so much light?

8. Start with a core. You can custom-tailor your resume quite easily if you have at least one core resume on your computer. That's your theme— and you can create a number of variations on it. Depending on your experience, you might prefer to have several core resumes. Each tells the truth about you, of course. But each emphasizes different facets of your experience.

For example, one core could be geared to customer service operations, which is something you have done and done well. Another resume features your marketing experience and accomplishments, while a third core emphasizes your consulting skills, which is another direction you could take.

9. Submit it *after* your meeting.[3] No resume you have prepared in advance could possibly be as good as one you would produce *after* you have met the decision maker. Prior to that, you really don't know exactly what their needs are, no matter how much advance research you have done.

10. Don't get too dependent on your resume. The biggest problem with resumes is that they tend to foster passivity. Job seekers think their resumes are work-horses—out there plowing the fields while they sit and wait for the phone to ring. That's more of a burden than we should place on any one piece of paper, or even two.

Which Format Is Best?

Should your resume be chronological, functional, or a combination? The format which is best for you is the one that allows you to present yourself most effectively.

- ◆ Chronological. Employers usually prefer this most popular format because it is easy to scan and understand. You can show a variety of experiences in one company as well as a progression of increasing responsibilities.
- ◆ Functional and combination formats cluster your experience, accomplishments, and skills in areas of competency, separate from your work history. These formats give you more freedom to emphasize your achievements while minimizing employment gaps. Functional and combination formats may be preferable for career changers, for those with limited work experience, and for people who have extensive volunteer work to their credit. They may also be better formats for people with excellent skills but less impressive job titles.

The functional format is organized by major skill areas. The work history section lists the positions held, including titles and names of the organizations, but does not detail the responsibilities.

The combination format is also organized by major skill area, but the work history section also describes responsibilities briefly. This format is particularly useful for describing the many hats that people in small organizations often wear.

EXAMPLES

Chronological

PHYLLIS MALLEY
17100 Elysian Way
Philadelphia, Pa. 19151
(215) 473-9760

OBJECTIVE: A position as a corporate consulting engineer

EXPERIENCE

American National Bank, Philadelphia, Pa.   **1986 to present**
A $24-billion diversified financial services company.

Operations Officer—1991 to present
Provided management consulting services to division managers.

- Reduced costs by 10% or $200,000 by analyzing organizational structures, staffing levels, and workflows of commercial loan operations division.
- Saved $222,000 by evaluating the statement-inserting function and recommending alternatives to purchasing new equipment.

Operations Analyst—1986 to 1991
Provided management consulting services to division managers.

- Recommended reducing branch staff expenses by 220% corporate-wide by utilizing a teller-staffing model.

Snelling Consulting Engineers, King of Prussia, Pa.   **1984–1986**
A national engineering consulting firm.

Industrial Engineer
Provided consulting services to clients, assisted in new client development and training of office personnel in use of IBM computers.

- Managed and performed field studies to improve productivity and quality of steel-processing operations.

The Culvert and Thompson Company, Philadelphia, Pa.   **1981–1984**
An apparel manufacturing company.

Facilities Manager

- Negotiated and supervised all contractual work for construction, roofing, and HVAC services.

PROFESSIONAL ASSOCIATIONS

Institute of Industrial Engineers, Financial Services Division, Philadelphia Chapter.

EDUCATION

BS., Industrial Engineering, University of Pennsylvania, 1981.

Chronological

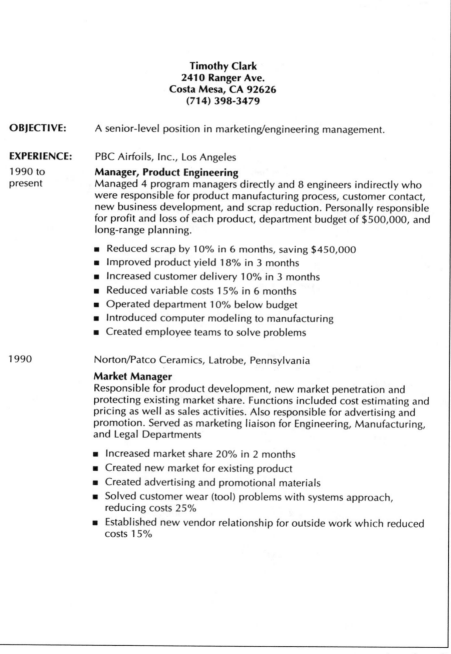

Timothy Clark
2410 Ranger Ave.
Costa Mesa, CA 92626
(714) 398-3479

OBJECTIVE: A senior-level position in marketing/engineering management.

EXPERIENCE: PBC Airfoils, Inc., Los Angeles

1990 to   **Manager, Product Engineering**
present   Managed 4 program managers directly and 8 engineers indirectly who
were responsible for product manufacturing process, customer contact,
new business development, and scrap reduction. Personally responsible
for profit and loss of each product, department budget of $500,000, and
long-range planning.

- Reduced scrap by 10% in 6 months, saving $450,000
- Improved product yield 18% in 3 months
- Increased customer delivery 10% in 3 months
- Reduced variable costs 15% in 6 months
- Operated department 10% below budget
- Introduced computer modeling to manufacturing
- Created employee teams to solve problems

1990   Norton/Patco Ceramics, Latrobe, Pennsylvania

Market Manager
Responsible for product development, new market penetration and
protecting existing market share. Functions included cost estimating and
pricing as well as sales activities. Also responsible for advertising and
promotion. Served as marketing liaison for Engineering, Manufacturing,
and Legal Departments

- Increased market share 20% in 2 months
- Created new market for existing product
- Created advertising and promotional materials
- Solved customer wear (tool) problems with systems approach,
  reducing costs 25%
- Established new vendor relationship for outside work which reduced
  costs 15%

(continued)

1977–1990   TRZ Inc., Valve Division, Cleveland, Ohio

Project Manager, 1987–1990
Responsible for ceramic tooling implementation for production use, new product development. Prepared business plan. Supervised the technical staff and served as liaison with production, engineering, and manufacturing.

- Reduced manufacturing costs by $2 million annually
- Developed a new business which later sold for $1.5 million
- Trained manufacturing personnel in new technology
- Transferred product from laboratory to production facility ahead of schedule and below budget

Manager, Technology Administration—1984–1988
Directed technology transfer to subsidiaries and affiliates worldwide in 12 countries. Managed royalty fee collection of $500,000 annually; initiated and followed up on items pertaining to intellectual property, patents, secrecy agreements, and technology licenses. Conducted training sessions to educate sales personnel on technical subjects and represented vice president of Engineering at group staff meetings.

- Increased turnaround time 50% in transfer of technology and flow of information
- Initiated plant expansion program of foreign affiliate
- Provided concept ideas and material for marketing
- Chaired worldwide technical conferences
- Served as technical consultant to foreign affiliates
- Helped establish joint venture company with Japanese affiliate
- Authored and published product design handbook

Product Engineer—1982–1984
Metallurgical Engineer—1977–1982

EDUCATION: Iowa State University, Ames, Iowa
       Master of Business Administration
       Master of Science, Metallurgical Engineering
       Bachelor of Science, Biology

Chronological

Keith Vanderbilt
7463 Highland Road   Chapel Hill, NC 27514   (919) 660-7731

SUMMARY

Management experience in designing and implementing marketing strategies for industrial products. Includes market analysis, sales channel management, pricing methods, and new product development.

WORK EXPERIENCE

Division Manager
American Process Co., Inc., Chapel Hill   **7/87-12/94**

Profit-loss responsibility for a division that markets production chemicals used by original equipment manufacturers.

- Restructured division's product line towards new, growth-oriented technologies;
- Increased sales by 51% and profitability by 63% over the past two years
- Created and implemented a sales channel strategy to sustain future growth.

Managed product development and roll-out, pricing, advertising, and overall strategy formation. Monthly reports of progress were presented to American Process Group directors.

Marketing Manager
Wesley Associates, Inc., Chapel Hill   **7/85-6/87**

- Developed nationwide network of manufacturer's representatives
- Refined pricing structure to correlate with product-line positioning
- Arranged a national account agreement with Mercedes-Benz Freightliner Truck Corp.

Entrepreneur
Vanderbilt Advertising Co., Chapel Hill   **Summer '83, '84**

- Conceived and developed advertising program that provided exposure for local service stations through door-to-door sales of maintenance coupons. Hired and trained sales staff. Earned approximately $15,000 each summer.

EDUCATION

B.A.: Duke University, August 1985
3.8 GPA in major (Business Administration)
3.4 overall; Dean's List 1984 and 1985

Functional

Carole Syms
10604 Knights Way
Royal Oaks, Colorado 80304
(303) 786-6435

OBJECTIVE

A senior-level position in Human Resource Management.

SUMMARY OF QUALIFICATIONS

- Policy development
- Compensation and benefits management
- Human resource information systems (HRIS)
- Relocations

- Health/wellness communications
- Performance appraisals
- EEO/AA
- Corporate travel
- Professional staff supervision

BUSINESS HISTORY

First Vice President, Human Resources
ROBERTS & CO. SECURITIES, INC.   **1989 to present**

Responsible for compensation/benefits planning and administration, HRIS, policy development, performance appraisal program, employee relations, professional staff supervision.

- Instrumental in establishing new, cost-effective company policies and procedures, including self-insured workers' compensation, corporate travel and relocation, tuition reimbursement, wellness programs, substance abuse.
- Converted manual record-keeping system to computerized database, effecting significant time savings; developed systems and security procedures; directed and trained staff.
- Created and implemented performance appraisal and job description programs for senior officers and exempt, sales, and nonexempt personnel.
- Implemented flexible benefits program company-wide.

Corporate Personnel Operations Manager
WORLDWIDE INDUSTRIAL CORPORATION   **Aug. 1984–Jan. 1989**

Responsible for policy and procedure development, national relocation program, HRIS system, and staff supervision.

- Computerized record-keeping system for 3,500 employees in four locations.
- Developed relocation policy; third-party service firm evaluations.
- Created policy manuals and handbook for four international company locations.

Personnel Supervisor
BANK TWO, Columbus, Ohio   **Feb. 1980–Aug. 1984**

Responsible for EEO/AA, employment, pension and benefits administration, policy development, employee counseling, staff supervision.

(continued)

EDUCATION

Bachelor of Arts, Business Administration. Graduated cum laude, Ohio State University

Continuous educational seminars in human resources including ADA, FMLLA, benefits, employment, HRIS, EEO/AA, relocation and employee assistance programs.

PROFESSIONAL ORGANIZATIONS

- Board of Trustees, Cleveland Society for Human Resource Management; past Vice President-Membership (1992-1994)
- Member, Columbus chapter of American Compensation Association
- Member, Columbus Relocation Roundtable and HR Systems Professionals

Functional

Sherry A. Wilcox
1085 Stonybrook Road
Springfield, New Jersey 07081-2548
(201) 376-7893

OBJECTIVE AND SUMMARY

Challenging position where analytical, communication, and team skills contribute to optimizing resource utilization. Special expertise in:

- Presentation/Communication
- Information Systems/Analysis
- International Business

- Team Leadership
- Negotiations
- Project Management

ACCOMPLISHMENTS

Communications:

- Selected to edit policy and procedures manual distributed to all unit managers to improve understanding of decentralized function. Reduced size of document 85% while enhancing clarity.
- Coached training staff on sensitive issues incorporated into management seminars.
- Co-developed management seminars.

Information Systems/Analysis:

- Redesigned departmental procedures using current automation tools to expedite work flow. Provided current work information and achieved cost avoidance of $100,000 annually through staff reduction.
- Projected required information flows for second-generation systems following initial period of rapid growth.
- Launched acceptance of minicomputers by managing first team to develop distributed data base system.
- Originated method to graphically present computer interfaces and flows. This project management tool used as standard by subsequent teams.
- Chosen to contribute systems support to world's largest private construction project. Project cost in excess of $7 billion.

International Business:

- Planned and managed transfer and utilization of sophisticated electronic equipment from the U.S. to an island in Indonesia.
- Negotiated 30% price reduction on software, breaking three-year deadlock for international negotiating team.

Team Leader:

- Headed multifunctional team of 8 professionals charged with developing unit managers' capabilities to interface appropriately with consultants. Avoided tax exposure.
- Led team negotiations to obtain (minimum) 116% price reduction and improved terms and conditions with maintenance vendor.

(continued)

Negotiations:

- Negotiated settlement of lease issues at less than 5% of original request. Avoided costly lawsuit.
- Advised and motivated sales representative for major supplier, strengthening business relationship and avoiding 10% cost increase from change to alternate supplier.
- Consolidated term agreements, reducing management effort 50%.

PROFESSIONAL EXPERIENCE

WORLDWIDE OIL, INC.   **1989–1992**
Supervisor, Contracts
Negotiated and managed broad range of contracts valued at $60 million annually. Strategized, solicited, and evaluated proposals for acquisition of services and capital equipment. Sold surplus assets.

Procurement Specialist, Technical   **1984–1988**
Negotiated and managed contracts valued at $5 million annually. Strategized, solicited, and evaluated proposals for acquisition of services and capital assets.

Supervisor, Systems Maintenance and Development   **1983–1984**
Managed computer support staff performing all requested computer functions for Materials Management.

Progressed from Junior Programmer to   **1968–1983**
Application Specialist/Design Coordinator

EDUCATION

MBA, Systems Approach to Management
State University of New York, Albany
BS, Mathematics, Economics
Rutgers University, New Brunswick, New Jersey

Functional

MAUREEN OWENS
2718 Century Road
Columbus, Ohio 43216-4097
(614) 481-5877

OBJECTIVE A position in accounting using strong analytical, organizational and problem-solving skills.

EXPERIENCE Bookkeeper (1992–1994)
Lakes Realty

- Maintained all records of accounts and related financial activity
- Evaluated credit reports
- Provided constructive recommendations that resulted in savings of approximately $45,000.

Administrator (1985-1990)
Every Day School, Columbus

- Increased enrollment 53% in 5 years
- Supervised school activities
- Hired and trained teachers
- Reorganized and computerized record-keeping system which enabled school to remain viable and thrive.

EDUCATION B.S. Accounting
and AWARDS Asheville College   Graduating May, 199x
GPA: 3.6

- Financial Executives Institute 1995 Academic Honors Award
- Honor Society
- Tax Institute Scholarship—for merit in accounting
- Tuition Equalization Scholarship—for merit
- Dean's Lists, 1992-95.

PROFESSIONAL ■ Treasurer—Accounting Association of Asheville College
AFFILIATIONS ■ Student Affairs Director—Institute of Management Accountants

COMPUTER Lotus 123, WordPerfect, dBase III, CRT IBM System 36

Functional

Robert B. Sanders
677 North Hayden Parkway
Washington, DC 20001
(202) 656-2453

OBJECTIVE AND QUALIFICATIONS SUMMARY

A program management position with a trade or professional organization.

- Strategic planning
- Leadership training
- Membership development

- Negotiations
- Fund raising
- Implementation

ACCOMPLISHMENTS

- Coordinated merger of two advocacy coalitions into single organization, resulting in at least $150,000 in savings and a more effective voice for both groups
- Increased member participation by 35% in two years
- Increased revenues by 23% in one year
- Designed and initiated strategic plan for continuing professional education for 30,000-member national organization
- Planned, implemented, and administered industry-wide standard-setting program that satisfied stringent Federal Trade Commission requirements for antitrust and restraint of trade regulations

EMPLOYMENT HISTORY

Accrediting Council for Training and Development   4/88–present
Washington, DC
Program Manager

Financial Planners Association of America   6/84–4/88
Washington, DC
Planning Associate

Mental Health Association for Metropolitan Boston   9/81–5/84
Boston, Mass.
Program Coordinator

EDUCATION

University of Virginia: B.S., Psychology
American Society of Association Executives: Certified Association Executive designation, 1985
Georgetown University: Twenty hours of graduate studies in business administration, 1980
U.S. Chamber of Commerce, Institutes for Organizational Management: 1975–78 (summers)

PROFESSIONAL ASSOCIATIONS

District of Columbia Society of Association Executives Foundation: Board Member and Treasurer, 1984–86

Combination

JoAnne M. Shearson
5400 Orchard Lane
Hudson, Ohio 44236
(216) 656-7984

OBJECTIVE

A position as an office manager.

SUMMARY OF QUALIFICATIONS

- Extensive experience in day-to-day office operations
- Strong organizational skills
- Developed and implemented financial controls
- Recruited and trained personnel
- Administered employee benefit programs

SUMMARY OF SKILLS

Organization/Administration

- Organized day-to-day operations of office
- Supervised and coordinated assignments and daily workflow for 100 legal secretaries
- Coordinated renovation of 30,000 square feet of office space
- Served on task force which evaluated and recommended integrated word processing/data processing equipment for centralized center and use at secretarial level

Personnel Administration

- Developed and implemented orientation program for new employees
- Automated insurance enrollment information to assure accuracy of reported information
- Assisted in development and implementation of performance appraisal program for all staff
- Served on task force which developed and evaluated job descriptions and compensation ranges for all staff positions

Financial Management

- Developed personal computer programs for use in preparation and monitoring of budget
- Created and implemented record-keeping procedures and forms for use in retirement plan administration

WORK HISTORY

Brandon, Bartlett, and Howe, L.P.A., Cleveland, Ohio
A general practice law firm with 30 employees
Office Manager   **1991 to present**
    Responsible for staff personnel, day-to-day office operations, and financial controls.

(continued)

Castle, Durant, & Leonard, Cleveland, Ohio
A national, multi-office law firm with 600 employees
Financial Analyst   **1982–1986**
   Coordinated preparation of operating and capital budgets for seven offices; monitored
   actual expenditures to budget on a monthly basis; administered five retirement plans
   with 500 participants.

Assistant to Controller   **1977–1983**
   Functioned as assistant office manager; evaluated and made recommendations for
   equipment acquisitions; prepared financial reports.

PROFESSIONAL ASSOCIATIONS

Association of Legal Administrators (national and local): vice president of local chapter
and member of newsletter staff

EDUCATION

Lakeland Community College—A.S. Secretarial Science (cum laude)

Supervisory Management Skills (two-year in-house education program), IBM PC,
Supercalc, and Lotus

REACHING HIRING AUTHORITIES WITH RESUMES

What's the Best Way to Do That?

That question may seem like a no-brainer. Doesn't everyone know that you mail your resume? You can do that, of course, as long as you don't send it out naked—that is, without a cover letter. You're never *that* rushed!

Your resume with a cover letter is the job search workhorse. The conventional wisdom is: get your resume into as many hands as possible, and the traditional way to do that is to mail it. That proves to everyone, including yourself, that you're trying hard to find employment. The most common job seekers' lament is variations on this theme:

"I sent out 35 resumes this week alone!"

OR

"I mailed 450 resumes in the last 6 months and received only 14 responses. They were all rejection letters!"

Mailing resumes seems safe. You're protected from the possibility of a painful face-to-face rejection. *Unfortunately, relying on mailed resumes will probably* prolong *your unemployment. The sooner you move beyond it, the sooner you'll be working!*

Job Search Rule #1: Don't Mail Your Resume to Local Employers![4]

Why not?

- Mailing your resume means that you will be reaching the organization, but not necessarily the hiring authority. Your resume will get to *someone* in the organization, but you have no control over *who* that might be. The human resources department or the decision maker's secretary could easily bury or discard your letter.

- Remember that *as a businessperson selling your services, you want to* make your presentation *(written, as well as in person)* to the person who can buy. *Making your presentation to anyone else is a waste of their time—and yours.*

- Even if your resume is appropriately addressed and "covered," it rarely gets the *kind of attention you want.* Employers are besieged with resumes. In smaller companies, they arrive by the dozens. Larger companies receive hundreds each day! What would *you* do if you received that many resumes?

◆ Whether you are applying for an advertised position or not, *resumes are used to screen people out, not in*, as has already been explained.

What Can You Do Instead?

With all these arguments against mailing out your resume, what can you do instead? If you feel you really must make it available, don't mail it. Drop it off in person. *Use the opportunity to get their attention and accomplish your objective: a face-to-face meeting with the decision maker!*

How can you do that? Be creative. And empathetic. For example, ask very courteously if it would be OK if you dropped off your resume. Emphasize that you don't want to interrupt their busy schedule and ask if you might bring it in just before the hour, like 7:55 a.m. or 11:55 a.m. By asking for 5 minutes *before* the hour, you're implying that you'll be there only 5 minutes. To alleviate their concern that you'll take too much time, you could promise not to take more than 2 minutes—or 5 minutes. Specify a number.

At the end of 2 minutes (or 5—whatever you have pledged), just smile and say: "I promised not to take more than "x" minutes and I'm keeping my word. But it looks like it would be a good idea to talk further and explore how I could help you and your company. Do you think we could get together next week, either Monday or Wednesday?"

Is it a crazy waste of time to go to someone's office for a 2-minute minute meeting? Not necessarily. *Even a 2-minute meeting is better than no meeting at all!* It allows you to become a *person*, rather than just a piece of paper or a disembodied voice. Remember, people hire people. Not pieces of paper. Or disembodied voices.

Not making your resume available until *after* your meeting is preferable. Perhaps you cannot mail your resume because:

◆ you are revising it

◆ you are changing careers and your resume only reflects what you *have* done, not what you *want to do*. And *can* do.

"Send me your resume" is usually interpreted as a sign of interest, but it is often the reverse. In Chapter 13, you'll learn to recognize it as an objection that you can overcome.

Resume Database Services

Through third-party resume database services, you can make your resume available to potential employers 24 hours a day, 7 days a week. These clearinghouses offer their client companies ongoing access to large numbers of resumes, helping these clients identify candidates who have specific credentials.[5] If you have a PC and modem, you can also insert your resume on appropriate bulletin boards on the Internet.

You cannot custom-tailor your resume to fit the needs of potential employers if you take these routes. But this high-tech scattershot approach can work for some job seekers, especially recent college grads with technical or other measurable skills. Regardless of your background, you may want to consider using one of the many services which, for a fee, will register you in their database for specific periods of time, usually three to six months. You should also find out what electronic services may be offered by your college or university.

Whether your resume arrives by E-mail or dog sled, more and more companies are scanning in your resume electronically. That means that the information on your resume is read and stored by computers. If your resume happens to contain the keywords that match their needs, like cellular biology or chemical etching procedures, you may be called for an interview.

But don't curl up for a nap, comforted by the vision of electronic robots whisking your resume to thousands of eager employers, impatient for the chance to hire you. Even if you are really lucky and an electronic match is made, you'll still have to convince human beings to offer you a job.

EMPLOYMENT INSURANCE CHECKLIST

✓ Does your resume explain what you are selling?

✓ And why they should hire you?

✓ Does it emphasize your accomplishments (which you have quanitified) and the benefits you will bring?

✓ Are you mailing your resume to local employers?

✓ Why?

✓ If you stop by with your resume, are you keeping your promise not to take more than "x" minutes?

✓ Are you targeting your resume to the hiring authority?

✓ Are you custom-tailoring your resume *after* your meeting?

CHAPTER 9

❖

Paper Chase Part 2: Letters, Etc.

LETTERS WITHOUT RESUMES

Getting the hiring authority's attention by mail can often be done better by letter without a resume. That may, in fact, be an interesting way to:

- ◆ answer ads
- ◆ approach employers unsolicited
- ◆ follow up on referrals

Pique Their Interest

Whether you're answering an ad, writing "cold," or following up on a suggestion from a referral, your letter must entice the recipient. It should be brief, professional, and so engaging that they'll be glad to hear from you when you follow up with a phone call. That cannot be done with a "one-size-fits-all" letter. It must be targeted to the needs of the individual recipient and that organization.

The following guidelines are appropriate for most letters that you will send.

1. Send it to a specific individual
2. Body of the letter

   - ◆ get their attention by indicating how you might benefit them
   - ◆ generate interest in meeting you
   - ◆ address a problem, if you know of one, or
   - ◆ ask a provocative question

3. Close/follow up

   - ◆ thank them for their consideration

- ◆ express interest in meeting them
- ◆ keep the initiative, write that you will call on a specific day
- ◆ then do it

To Answer Ads

Refer to the ad and make a list of their requirements. Then, list your relevant credentials, item by item.

Example:

Payroll Manager

Our dynamic, fast-growing retail company has an extraordinary opportunity for a dynamic, goal-oriented Payroll Manager.

They Want	Your Qualifications
◆ dynamic, goal-oriented	◆ dynamic, goal-oriented
◆ 5+ yrs. proven managerial experience in personnel/payroll administration and processing.	◆ 4 1/2 years of proven managerial experience in personnel/payroll administration and processing.
◆ Expert with ADP and Report Writer.	◆ Expertise in ADP and Report Writer
◆ Exceptional communication, problem-solving skills.	◆ Excellent communication, problem-solving skills. Experienced in supervising, reviewing, auditing staff, etc. etc. etc.
◆ Responsibilities: supervising reviewing, auditing all salary and hourly bi-weekly payroll processing.	
◆ Previous experience with 401K and Section 125 implementation is extremely important.	
◆ Experience with POS systems is a plus.	

Your message is: I have what you want. Write that you will call at a certain time to set up an appointment. And do it. Don't wait for them to call.

If you don't have *exactly* what they want, reply to the ad anyway. Remember, their list of requirements is really a *wish* list. They want 3 to 5 years of experience in rhinoceros-riding and you have only 2? Explain that your accomplishments in those two years were exceptional. For example, you are experienced in guiding people on rhinoceros riding safaris, the very business they are getting into. Or you have compensating assets, like your year with Crocodile Capers, where you successfully guided several groups on virtual vacations. (For more about compensating assets, see Chapter 13.)

Personalize Your Letter

If the ad advises you to send your resume to the human resources department, call and get the name of the department head and address your letter to that individual. If you're answering a newspaper box number ad, you could start with Dear Human Resources Manager or the much livelier greeting: "Good Morning!"

Can the Post Office Help?

If the ad lists a post office box number, you can find out who rented that box by calling the local U.S. Postal Service box rental department. Having that information will help you respond appropriately. If you are employed, be very cautious about blind ads, if you respond at all. It could be the company you work for that is advertising.

Approach an Organization "Cold"

Don't hesitate to contact organizations even if you don't have a personal referral. Use the basic formula, emphasizing how you might be able to benefit them. You don't know if you can, but you would like to meet them to explore that possibility. Your research is particularly important here.

Example:

January 17, 19xx

Mr. Fred Focil
Focil Facsimiles
99 Framingham Way
Framingham, MA 02587

Dear Mr. Focil:

I have read the article in the January 16 issue of the *Swampscott Daily* about your company's new ancient artifact program. As Director of Development for the Dinosaur Egg Manufacturing Company, I created a program which increased our egg production by 33% in less than three years.

Because we have had such excellent results, I believe my experience could be beneficial to you and your colleagues at Focil Facsimiles.

Your consideration is very much appreciated. I will call on Monday, January 22, to arrange for a meeting and am looking forward to our discussion.

Sincerely,

(signed) T. Rex

Here's another example of approaching an organization without a personal referral:

March 23, 19xx

Mr. E. T. Green, President
Dandiest Dandelions Unlimited
1 Growers Way
Bloomington, Ind. 78435

Dear Mr. Green:

Having just returned from the March meeting of the Dandelion Growers of America, I am aware that Dandiest is the industry leader—on the cutting edge of dandelion growing in the U.S. The progress you and your team have made at Dandiest is really impressive.

As I understand it, Dandiest faces the same problem as all the other dandelion growers: distribution. Would you be interested in a new packaging material that would greatly reduce the cost of dandelion distribution?

My specialty is dandelion packaging, and I have developed a new method which I think you would find very attractive. That's one of the reasons I believe I could be very helpful to you and your colleagues at Dandiest. I will call on Thursday, March 31, to set up an appointment and look forward to meeting with you soon.

Sincerely,

(signed) May Flowers

Follow Up on Referrals

Your networking has generated lots of suggestions for people you could contact. Having asked permission to use their names, you're ready to follow up. Calling, rather than writing and then calling, is preferable because it is faster. If your network contact suggested that you write first, however, do that. But don't enclose a resume unless you were urged to do so.

Your letter begins by referring to the person who suggested that you make the contact. Include some background about yourself and close with a statement about how you will follow up. Since you're depending on your contact's influence to ease your passage into their office, keep this letter short. The guidelines offered below suggest a slight modification of your basic letter.

1. Send it to the individual, mentioning your contact's name and organization (if appropriate).
2. The body of the letter should

   ◆ Indicate (if appropriate) why your contact suggested that you get in touch with them, being diplomatic in your description. For example, you're an office manager and your friend referred you to the executive VP of Beanbag Furniture stores because he knows that their office manager just married Mr. Beanbag and quit her job. "The Beanbags are cruising in the Caribbean and I hear the office is in total disarray," your friend explained. You would, of course, be very circumspect and simply indicate that you were advised that you might be helpful at this time.

   ◆ State how they might benefit from meeting you, but keep this brief.

3. Close, as described above.

COVER LETTERS

If your job search covers a large geographical area, you will have to mail your resume. And you'll need to cover it with a strong letter. Many employers consider cover letters more important than resumes and read them more carefully. In addition to the points made above, be sure your letter complements, but does not repeat, your resume. Cover letters offer an opportunity to demonstrate your creativity, and if you are in public relations, advertising, etc., you'll probably enjoy that challenge.

Sample Cover Letters

The specific wording depends, of course, on whether this letter and resume are being sent in response to an ad, "cold" to an organization, or following up on a referral's suggestion. The relevant formulas would apply.

Sample Response to an Out-of-State Ad

October 15, 19xx

Ms. Helen Travers, Vice President
Human Resources
Feel Good Pharmaceuticals
Morristown, NJ 07864

Dear Ms. Travers:

Your ad in the October 13 issue of the *Wall Street Journal* for a payroll manager intrigued me because it sounds as though it was written for me.

As you can see from my resume, I have the communication, problem-solving, and other skills and experience that you are looking for. Happily, my four years of payroll management experience includes implementing 401K Section 125 programs, which the ad indicates is particularly important to you. What my resume cannot communicate, of course, is my diligence and dedication to excellence.

I am confident that I can do the job and would like to meet with you to explore this matter further. I appreciate your consideration and will call next Friday to see if there is any additional information you would like to have.

Sincerely,

Bernard Taylor

"Cold" Out-of-State Letter

August 20, 19xx

Ms. L. Muffit, VP, Sales
Spiderweb Mills
8 Spinning Circle
Webber, Fla. 34236

Dear Ms. Muffit:

The August issue of *Spinning and Weaving* described Spiderweb Mills's planned expansion to the Far East. I am intrigued by the idea of selling silk to China and believe I could be very helpful to you.

For the past seven years, I have sold cotton to Egypt and my sales have increased at least 11% every year, as my resume indicates. Since I speak Chinese fluently and know the culture well, I am certain that I could be a real asset to you and Spiderweb Mills in your new exporting venture.

I sincerely appreciate your attention and will call next Tuesday to arrange for a meeting.

Yours truly,

(signed) Lee Wong

Letter to Referral

June 14, 19xx

Mr. Lawrence Howard, President
Howard and Associates
576 Norton Blvd.
Charlotte, NC 28227

Dear Mr. Howard:

Jerry Shaw suggested that I contact you and show you some samples of the writing and editing work I have done at Deep Six Publishing.

As the copy editor of *Fishing Facts and Fantasy*, I have had the satisfaction of seeing our magazine move from conception to reality and attain a circulation of 19,000. We are very pleased with the excellent response from our readers and the many favorable comments we hear in the trade.

Since Jerry was aware that we're starting a new publication for pheasant fanciers, he thought it would be a good idea for us to get together. I would certainly like to do that and will call on Monday to see when you might be available for a meeting.

Best wishes,

(signed) Melissa Cartwell

SPECIALIZED MAIL

Should You Fax Your Resume or Letter?

If you are asked to fax your resume or letter long distance, do it. But for local contacts, you probably don't want fuzzy print on low-quality paper to represent you, especially in your first contact with a prospective employer. If your resume is unsolicited, it might get the attention of the person you are addressing. But it could also be considered junk mail and quickly discarded.

Is E-Mail the Best Route?

E-mail is rapidly replacing traditional mail for millions of people. It is significantly faster and more convenient, and job bulletin boards are becoming increasingly common. Few job seekers are sending their resumes via E-mail, however, although that will undoubtedly change in the near future. There are some concerns about confidentiality with E-mail which could be a problem, especially if you are employed.

Telegrams

If the mail and phone are not opening the door for you, you might try this approach. It's expensive, but so is unemployment. Example:

Dear Ms. Grabapple:

Have tried to reach you for 2 weeks. Believe I can help you with your new planting program. Would appreciate your call: John E. Appleseed (987) 123-4567.

A more humorous approach, which might not be for everyone, could be something like this:[1]

Dear Ms. Grabapple:

Have been trying to reach you for 2 weeks. There's good news and bad news. To find out what the good news is, call me! To find out what the bad news is, call me! John E. Appleseed (987) 654-3210.

WHAT ABOUT NUMBERS?

Mass Mailings?

Since we have emphasized the importance of contacting large numbers of potential employers, mass mailings or broadcast letters might seem to be ideal. Using your computer, your SIC code, and the names of appropriate executives in relevant companies that are listed in various directories, you could send individually addressed letters to every employer who could possibly hire you. There might be hundreds, even thousands, in your area alone! That sounds efficient, but in our experience, mass mailings really only benefit the firms in the addressing and mailing business.

How Many Letters Should You Send?

Only as many as you can follow up within a few days. Your letter should indicate that you will be calling on a certain day or part of the week. Then *do it!* Without a follow-up call, your letter is not worth mailing!

Why? Remember that reaching a hiring authority via the mail is really a 3-step process:

1. mail
2. follow-up phone call to set up appointment
3. meeting

Be sure you know what you want to accomplish at each step of the way. If you focus on the specific objective, you're more likely to accomplish it. And you're more likely to avoid getting bogged down with unrealistic expectations.

◆ The purpose of your letter is to make the hiring authority more receptive to talking with you, to "warm up" your follow-up call. (The disadvantage, of course, is that he has time to come up with reasons not to talk with you—or see you.)

◆ The objective of your phone call is to set up a meeting.

You can condense the 3-step process into 2-steps by dispensing with the initial letter. Simply call.

USING THE TELEPHONE TO REACH THEM (without prior mailing)

Compared to the mail, the phone has several advantages because it:

◆ reaches the appropriate person
◆ gets his or her attention
◆ is fast
◆ is interactive: provides immediate feedback
◆ (one call) may be all you need to schedule a meeting with a hiring authority!

The flip side? You must be ready. That means more planning and preparation, which is described in the next several chapters.

EMPLOYMENT INSURANCE CHECKLIST

✓ Are your letters targeted to specific individuals?
✓ Do they indicate how you might be able to benefit them?
✓ Are you answering ads?
✓ Are you following up on referrals' suggestions?
✓ Are you contacting organizations "cold"?
✓ Do your letters pique their interest in you?
✓ Are you following up every letter with phone calls?

C H A P T E R   1 0

Make the Telephone Your Friend

Finding employment without using the telephone is like flying a plane without instruments. It's almost impossible. You can use the phone to get information about *them*—employers, the industry, specific companies, and hiring authorities. And you can find out who needs it—which company needs your services? The phone is also an excellent way to contact decision makers and persuade them to meet you.

Since you'll be using your phone, why not make it your friend? Your telephone line is, literally, the shortest line between you and your next employer.

PHONE PHOBIA

Common Concerns

Despite its obvious importance, using the telephone to find employment makes grown men blanch. Calling strangers is particularly unnerving.

Why? Several former executives, participants in outplacement workshops, explained that they:

- don't know how to manage the whole process
- can't get past the secretary
- fear that other person won't want to talk
- hate waiting for return calls
- are uncomfortable with strangers
- fear unknown questions
- feel like they're invading the other person's privacy
- don't like to ask for help

What's the Worst That Could Happen?

All of these concerns, which are understandable, will be addressed in this and subsequent chapters. First, let's put these anxieties in perspective. These same people were asked: What's the worst thing that could happen? The most horrific fate anyone could imagine is: *The person I was calling might hang up!*

Q. "Has that ever happened to you?"

A. Negative head shaking.

Q. "Do you think it *would* happen?"

A. More negative body language.

Q. "If it *did* happen—the worst-case scenario—*could you live with that?*"

A. Everyone smiled.

If you are really worried about the worst-case scenario, imagine having that experience. Write about how you think you'd feel. Then set that paper aside. If you look at telephoning objectively, it's hardly a hazardous activity. There's *no* way to lose financially. The risks are all psychological. *Feeling a lack of control. Fear of rejection.* What about the risks of doing nothing and continued unemployment?

MANAGING THE WHOLE PROCESS

Overview

We've pointed out that what separates you from your next job is inadequate information. Nowhere is this more apparent than in the use of the phone. And nowhere is the risk/reward ratio more dramatic. To help you learn to use the phone effectively, the process is explained in detail. This chapter includes:

- Know who you are calling
- What is your strategy?
- What is the purpose of your call?
- Mechanics of phoning
  - Best times to call
  - When not to call

Subsequent chapters explain:

- How to bypass the gatekeeper
- What message do you leave?
- Telephone body language
- What do you say to the hiring authority?
- How do you respond to probable objections?
- How do you obtain appointments?
- How do you follow up?
- Summary: How can you make each call productive?

HOW DO YOU START?

Know Who You Are Calling

You're looking for a position in corporate lending and you've already researched some of your target companies and prioritized them into A, B, and C companies. Let's say you would give your right arm to work for the Sandy Banks Bank. You've researched SBB at the library, obtained their annual report, and have identified B. Good, VP for corporate lending, as your hiring authority. All this information is in your tickler file.

What Is Your Strategy?

If the Sandy Banks Bank is not advertising for people in corporate lending, how can you begin? One option is to start by contacting their competitors. These are, in fact, your "C" companies, like the Shifting Dunes Bank and First National Piggy Bank.

By talking with the competition, you can learn about what's going on in the industry as well as practice your interviewing skills. Then, when you approach Sandy Banks, your A-priority company, you're a much more impressive candidate—better informed and more confident.

What Is the Purpose of Your Call?

1. *When you're calling a hiring authority, your purpose is clear: a face-to-face meeting. Nothing less will do.* If you are not calling a hiring authority, you might want either:

- ◆ a meeting or
- ◆ a phone conversation

Most job seekers choose the latter. It's an efficient, inexpensive way to get information. But face-to-face meetings with network contacts are often more valuable because:

- ◆ You *become* a person.
- ◆ Some bonding will probably occur.
- ◆ This could be the beginning of a business friendship.
- ◆ Information is more readily shared.
- ◆ You may be introduced to others in the company when you're there.
- ◆ You get visible information about the company, possibly a tour of their facility, etc.
- ◆ These meetings are more memorable for both parties and potentially have more long-range consequences. The more you know about the individual and the organization, the better your chances of developing a working relationship.
- ◆ This person could have input into hiring decisions or might become a hiring authority in the future.

2. If your objective is *not* a meeting, it's information:

- ◆ about that company
- ◆ the industry
- ◆ the kind of work that person does
- ◆ names of others who might be helpful.

Make each call productive. The following formula, easy to remember as the AAA formula, can help you do that.

- ◆ Ask for the information you wish, such as the names of others in the field that you might talk with. For example:

  "Do you know anyone else in electronics who might be able to talk with me?"

◆ Appreciate whatever help/suggestions they give you.

"That's a great suggestion. I've heard they're really doing well at EE. I'll call Mr. Short and Ms. Circuit right away."

◆ Ask for permission to use their name.

"May I use your name when I call? Thanks so much! I really appreciate your help."

To Call or Not to Call: The Mechanics of Phoning

When do you call? Are there *good* days? *Bad* days? *Good* times? *Bad* times?

Use your knowledge. And empathy. Some industries and occupations have particularly busy seasons or times of the day. Respect those. If your daily newspaper has a 3:00 p.m. deadline each afternoon, 2:30 p.m. is not a great time to call the editor. But don't make too many assumptions about *bad* times. Not everyone's out to lunch at noon. Some people *are* working the week after Christmas. In fact, some job seekers have found that the holiday season is an excellent time to make calls to businesspeople. As one outplaced manager observed:

"At least they're in town. And because they're less rushed, they're more willing to meet you."

Try calling executives early (7:30 a.m.- 9:00 a.m. or even earlier if you know that's their schedule), during lunch hours, and after 5:00 p.m. They're more likely to answer the phone themselves when their secretaries are away.

What's the *best* time to call someone? *Now!* The best day? *Today*—even if it is Good Friday or the day before Thanksgiving. There is no one-size-fits-all answer, except this:

◆ *Ask* what are the best times to reach that person.

◆ *Keep calling until you do.*

Your persistence and flexibility will give you a big edge at meetings, too. The head of one small manufacturing company, for example, offers to meet job seekers at 6:30 a.m. He claims it's his best time. It's also a quick and easy way for him to "separate the sheep from the goats. *If they cannot accommodate me when they're looking for work, what good would they be on the job?*"

EMPLOYMENT INSURANCE CHECKLIST

✓ When you telephone, what's the worst thing that can happen?
✓ Can you live with that?
✓ Do you know who you are calling?
✓ What is the purpose of your call?
✓ Are you calling a hiring authority?
✓ Are you seeking a meeting or information?
✓ Are you getting something from each call?
✓ What is the best time to call?

CHAPTER 11

❖

Gliding Past the Gatekeeper

How do I get past the secretary? It's a question that keeps cropping up among job seekers. If you feel you've got to put on a suit of armor to get past fire-breathing gatekeepers, you're probably not going to make too many calls.

And that's what happens. Intimidated by gatekeepers (and the rest of the phoning process), job seekers don't make enough calls. As a result, they put their job search "on hold." And that's sad, because most secretaries are just trying to do their jobs. Understanding their needs, being well prepared, and treating the secretary with courtesy and respect can go a long way towards accomplishing what you want—a chance to talk with the hiring authority.

GATEKEEPERS' PERSPECTIVE

Let's look at your call from their perspective. One of their responsibilities is to identify and screen callers. Before they'll put your call through, they'll almost invariably request some basic information.

Three Screening Questions[1]

1. Your name?
2. Who (what organization) are you with?
3. What is the nature of this call?

If you're prepared with good answers to these three questions, you'll probably get through to the boss. If you aren't, you won't.

Treat Everyone with Respect

Too often, secretaries and receptionists are not given the consideration they deserve. (It's only when they're gone and the office comes to a standstill that everyone realizes how indispensable they are.) One way to show respect is to use that person's name. Secretaries often identify themselves when they answer the phone. If they don't, ask and make a note of it. Using their names will also help you establish rapport.

BE PREPARED: KNOW *WHAT* TO SAY

Answer the Questions Honestly and Succinctly

1. **Your name?** That's easy. "My name is Kathy Kumquat." Sometimes, you can add a bit of humor and make your message memorable. Michael Woczejnhowski did that with a twinkle in his eye. Empathizing with strangers who were struggling to pronounce his name, he advises: "Just say: Where's your house key? That's close enough."

2. **Who are you with?** That's more challenging, especially if you've lost your job. Options?

   ◆ You can continue to identify yourself with your former employer:

      "I was with Quirky Controls until May." That's correct, of course, but you're communicating that you are no longer employed. And the danger is that you'll be switched immediately to human resources.

   ◆ If you have set yourself up as a consultant, you would use the name of the consulting company.

      "I'm Ronald Robust with Ronald Robust and Associates." Or, "I'm self-employed."

   ◆ If you are not a consultant, you can simply say:

      "I'm with myself," or "I'm not with anyone."

3. What is the nature of this call? Some people say, "This is a personal matter." But is it? *Employment is clearly a business matter.* Suggesting that it's something else is simply not honest. And it could easily backfire. Just think how you would respond if someone called and said it was a personal matter when it clearly was not. Could you ever trust that person again?

- ◆ **There's a better approach.** It's simple. And honest. Use a general word which describes their—and your—business or activity.

   For example, if you're in development and you're calling the VP for development, your call is about "*development*." If you're a leasing specialist, your call is about "*leasing*." A systems engineer is calling about "*systems engineering*."

   Some of these generic terms are particularly powerful door openers. For example, if you're an accountant calling about "*auditing*," brace yourself! You can expect really fast action!

Why not confide in the secretary? Couldn't you explain that you're looking for a job and ask for her help? That may work in some cases. But, in general, you'll use your time most productively by making your presentations to decision makers. Secretaries may have input into hiring decisions, but they are rarely hiring authorities.

Confiding in others might not only waste your time, it could be counterproductive. The secretary, for example, might explain that the company is not hiring (which, as far as she knows, is correct), and connect you to human resources. They'll tell you the same thing. The result? You haven't reached the decision maker and you've reduced your chances of doing so.

Four "Magic" Words[2]

You've answered the three screening questions. Now, you want to be connected. You are, of course, *invariably polite. No* hint of arrogance. But you want action. This is not a plea. You *expect* to be connected!

You can communicate that very well with four "magic" words: *put me through, please.* Thousands of job seekers, including gatekeepers, can attest to its effectiveness.

Timing

Put me through, please is most effective when used **immediately** after you have answered a question. Don't hesitate! That could give the secretary time to come up with additional questions. Practice so that you eliminate those "uhs" and "ums." Keep coming back to **put me through, please** until you're connected.

Putting That All Together

Here's an example of how you can use this formula to get past the gatekeeper (GK):

Ring . . . ring.

GK: "Hello. Drawbridge & Company."

You: *"Hello. This is Horatio Houdini. Put me through to Cheryl Castle, please."*

GK: "Who are you with, Mr. Houdini?"

You: *"I'm with myself. Put me through to Cheryl Castle, please."*

GK: "And what is this call about, Mr. Houdini?"

You: "It's about magic" (or organizational development or MIS or physical therapy—whatever your field is).

Preempting the Three Questions

Since you know which questions you will be asked, why not answer them *before* they're asked? Preempting the questions has two advantages:

1. You'll sound *authoritative* and are, therefore, more likely to get connected.
2. You'll probably *save time*. Example:

"This is Wendy Workout with Wendy Workout Aerobics. I'm calling Jane Fonda about exercise programs. Put me through, please."

How will the secretary respond? You have already answered the questions she was planning to ask. She may ask them again, in which case you respond politely:

"As I said, this is Wendy Workout. I'm with Wendy Workout Aerobics and I'm calling Jane Fonda about an exercise program. Put me through, please."

Or she'll simply connect you.

BE PREPARED: KNOW *HOW* TO SAY IT

Your Tone Communicates More Than Your Words

How *you speak is the most critical component of your message—it communicates more than **what** you say*. After you've answered the three basic questions and have asked to be connected, few secretaries will probe further *if your manner is as convincing as your words*.

Ideally, your words and tone of voice are businesslike, communicating the expectation that you'll get what you want. Your request is stated in a way that gives the secretary direction and does not leave room for too much discretion.

By conveying assurance and conviction, you're not only more likely to get through to the decision maker. You're more likely to persuade that person to meet you.

Body Language

You're more likely to be persuasive if your body, as well as your mind, is well positioned. Relax. Good posture helps you breathe easily and relax your muscles. Lean forward slightly, with uncrossed arms and legs in an open posture, receptive to what the other person is saying. It's the same "good listening" posture you use in face-to-face meetings.

Phone conversations shut out visible cues—the other person's eyes and facial expressions—which tell you so much about what they're thinking. That forces you to listen even more carefully. When you do, you can *"hear"* the body language. Tense muscles, a tight mouth, and hunched posture result in a strained voice. So keep your mirror nearby—and smile!

What do you sound like? *How* you sound, as well as *what* you say, will make the crucial first impression on the person you call. Have you ever listened to yourself on the telephone? Try taping a conversation with a friend, explaining what you're doing, of course. The sound of your own voice may surprise you. Is it pleasing? Too soft? Too loud? Nasal? Boring? Energetic?

What about the pace of your conversation? And your diction? Should you slow down a bit? Pause between thoughts and sentences so that it is easier for others to follow you? Are you talking too much?

Write It! Then Practice, Practice, Practice!

Write out your answers to the 3 screening questions. Then tape it. Role play with a friend. Revise and rehearse until you feel comfortable and sound convincing, *not* "canned."

Then, do a reality check. Call 3 companies. Any companies. If you're not getting past the secretary, revise your script and practice. When you do, you'll probably be amazed, like participants in Sale to Success telephone labs, by how quickly you get past the gatekeeper. Participants simply answered the 3 screening questions authoritatively, then said the "magic" words: *Put me through, please.* Presto! They were talking with the decision maker!

Meetings and Messages

"She's in a Meeting"

The person you're calling is never *"in."* She's either *in a meeting* or *on another line.* What's the best way to handle that?

Put on your Sherlock Holmes hat! Ask the secretary when she would advise you to call back. Be very appreciative. Take notes. And follow through.

If she's on another call, you might avoid more telephone tag by holding briefly, perhaps mentioning to the secretary that you'll hold for half a minute while you do some work. But *don't give the impression that you have all day*. You don't. Be sure to *communicate that you're busy and your time is valuable. You are. And it is!*

What Message Do You Leave?

Waiting for *them* to call back is never fun. When you're unemployed, it's not only terribly disheartening, it's counterproductive. If you're expecting a call, you'll hesitate to use the phone. That puts your job search "on hold" and wastes your valuable time.

In fact, you don't *want* them to call you back. *You* want to do the calling. Why? Remember that you are—or soon will be—calling at least ten people every day. Picture this. You've had a good start this week—called 22 people on Monday and Tuesday. Now, it's Wednesday and you're getting ready for an appointment. Just as you step out of the shower, you hear the phone and pick it up. A voice says, "It's Sue Namie returning your call."

"Sue Namie," you repeat, trying frantically to remember which company she's with. And who referred you. "Yes," she continues, sensing your hesitation. "Sue Namie from Tsunami Insurance. I have a message that you called."

By now, you've caught your breath. But you still don't remember who referred you to Sue Namie. Wrapped in your wet towel, you scramble to find your notes. But by the time you do, it's too late. You have lost those precious few seconds when you could have sounded confident and well organized. It's a cliche, but it's true: *You have only one chance to make a good first impression.* That's just as true on the phone as it is in person.

Why risk it? There are so many elements in your job search that you can't control. But you *can* manage this. *You can take charge simply by calling when you're ready. Not before! And you'll avoid the "Waiting-for-the-telephone-to-ring blues."*

The message you should leave: your name, but not your phone number. Why leave your name? You want the other person to remember it. After your 43rd call, she'll be curious. Who is this Humphrey Humperdink, anyway?

Preparation and polite persistence pay. You can convert the secretary into an ally by respecting her and helping her do her job. Be prepared. Practice. Then call! Expect to be connected. *Put me through, please,* stated authoritatively after you have answered the three screening questions, will work. You'll be connected to the decision maker.

Now, what should you say? Read on!

EMPLOYMENT INSURANCE CHECKLIST

✓ How can you show respect to gatekeepers?
✓ How can you help them do their jobs?
✓ Are you prepared to respond to their 3 screening questions?
✓ Are you using the 4 "magic words"?
✓ Have you listened to yourself on tape?
✓ Role-played with a friend?
✓ Did you glide past the gatekeeper?
✓ Do you know what message to leave?
✓ What's the best day to call?
✓ What's the best time to call?

CHAPTER 12

❖

You're *On*:
Now What Do You Say?

NOT *"Hello. Are you hiring?"* That desperate call of the wild is heard by companies every day. But not usually by decision makers. They're more likely to be persuaded by messages that take their interests into account.

ANALYZE THE SITUATION

Focus on What They're Thinking

You know what you want: a meeting with the hiring authority. The best way to accomplish that is to focus on them and what they're thinking. Prospective employers are, in fact, potential buyers (of your services). When you ask for a few minutes of their time, you are also asking them to make a buying decision. The cost? Their valuable time.

Their Unspoken Questions and Your Answers

Let's look at your approach in terms of:

- ◆ *Questions:* Theirs (unspoken)
- ◆ *Answers:* Yours

Q. **Why** should he talk with you?

A. Because you're making him aware of his problem or need and your possible solution.

Q. **What** is his problem or need?

A. You have researched your target companies and know something about their needs. Your approach could also be based on some reasonable assumptions: They want to make and save money, look

◆ 147 ◆

good, etc. By listening carefully, you'll learn more about what they want.

Q. How can you help him resolve this difficulty?

A. Having solved similar problems, you are confident that you have the relevant knowledge, ability, and experience to help them if you have sufficient information.

Q. Why should he trust you?

A. You're demonstrating your knowledge and integrity.

Q. Why *should he agree to meet you?*

A. *Because there may be something in it for him: The benefits outweigh the costs. He sees this meeting as a good investment of his time.*

ABCs of the APPROACH[1]

What You Do	*What He's Thinking*
1. Attract hiring authority to self, services; get his attention; make him aware of lack or need.	Becomes AWARE of lack or need.

2. Build Belief in you through Benefits you may be able to provide. Your accomplishments offer proof.	Believes (logically):
	   He can use IT
	   IT's worth the cost
	   He can afford IT
	   Believes (emotionally)
	     that he wants it.

3. Close. Ask for a commitment.	Commits to IT.

How Can You Accomplish Your Objective?

What You Must Do

1. Get his attention

   ◆ *Arouse his curiosity*

   ◆ *Build that curiosity into genuine interest*[2]

2. Make him aware of a problem or need (if necessary)

   ◆ *You must perceive the other person as someone with a need*

   ◆ *You can help meet that need*

3. Present possible benefits to him

   ◆ Solutions you may be able to provide
   ◆ Your accomplishments provide evidence

4. Close for an appointment: Get a commitment of time.

The First Order of Business: Get His Attention!

Your marketing plan asks: How can you reach them? That means not only connecting physically but also getting their attention, whether you're using a referral or calling "cold."

Example: You've had 11 years of experience with automatic teller machines. The company you're calling, Out-of-Order ATM, manufactures ATMs. There's no advertised opening. But business seems to be thriving—you've seen Out-of-Order ATMs all over the place. So you think it's safe to assume that, even though they're not actively recruiting, they have unmet needs.

Ms. Pin, the VP for sales, is busy at her desk, surrounded by papers and reports. She's preparing for a regional sales meeting on Friday. Sales are not as strong as they had planned, but she's hoping that their new virtual banking ATMs will really start to move this next quarter.

Like anyone else you might call, Ms. Pin is immersed in her own world—her thoughts, hopes, and anxieties. It's the same *"barrier of preoccupation,"*[3] a kind of cocoon or layer of absorption, that separates each of us from the rest of the world.

If you want her to listen to you, you must break through that barrier. Because the phone, unlike the mail, commands attention, it can be an extremely effective instrument for getting through that barrier. But not for long!

You must say something that will *so* whet her appetite, arouse her curiosity, and stimulate her interest that she will listen.[4] *And you have only a few seconds to do it!*

What do you do? Using a variation of an approach developed by the late Jack Gubkin, you **GRAB** *her attention—with the letters in GRAB spelling out the process:*

G—Greet her in a warm and friendly manner.

R—Refer to a friend or mutual acquaintance, if appropriate.

A—Attract attention to her problem/need and your possible solution and Ask for a meeting to explore what you can do for them.

B—Build Belief (in you): Emphasize your *Best Benefit* (for her).

Let's look at these four elements more closely.

G. Greeting. A pleasant, friendly greeting should be easy.

- ◆ Introduce yourself.
- ◆ Use her name, being sure to pronounce it correctly.
- ◆ Keep it short.

"Good morning, Ms. Pin. My name is Dan Deposit."

OR

"Good morning, Ms. Pin. I'm Dan Deposit with Dan Deposit and Associates."

R. Referrals. Many job seekers believe that referrals have almost magical properties, so they spend a disproportionate amount of time and energy getting referrals. They can, of course, warm up an otherwise "cold" call. But sooner or later, you'll have to explain why the other person should spend time with you. There are, unfortunately, no abracadabras that will open decision makers' doors, but some names will work better than others:

"My friend, Dan Rather, suggested that I call you."

OR

"Connie Chung thought we should get together."

A. Attract Attention to Her Problem/Need. The more you know about their problem or need, the more persuasive you're likely to be. Your research will pay off here, especially if you cannot claim impressive achievements. Knowing something about them can give you an opening:

"I just read in the Bank Account Weekly *that Out-of-Order ATMs is introducing new virtual banking ATMs. I'll bet your sales take off like a rocket and you just might need some help. Don't you think you could use a bright, energetic young person with very good computer skills like me? I know I could do a very good job for you in sales support. Could we get together either Thursday or Friday to discuss how I might be able to help you?"*

Asking a provocative (not a controversial) question is another way to get their attention. A public relations specialist might say:

"You're probably familiar with the big Pasty Pasta campaign that we did this year. Pasty's market share has increased 6% already. Would you be interested in enhancing your company's visibility through some very original promotions?"

OR

"Would you be interested in some innovative ways to enhance your company's professional image in the community?"

If you're answering an ad by phone, you have to pass the test to get an appointment. The same rules apply here as when you're responding by mail. The message you want to communicate is: *You have what they're looking for.* You must, of course, be honest and not fake knowledge. If they want to know about your experience, your response is something like this:

"From what I understand from your ad for a data processing coordinator, you're looking for a person with experience in computer hardware, software, and applications systems, is that right? In my previous position with a proprietary school, I was able to get all their records organized on the IBM AS 400, which I believe is the machine you use, so that their registrations in September were accomplished in about half the time it had taken previously. Is that the kind of person you're looking for? (Wait for an answer.) *Good! Then why don't we get together to discuss how I can help you? Would either Thursday afternoon or Friday morning be convenient for you?"*

OR

"Your ad for a stunts person says that you're looking for someone with experience in jumping through blazing hoops. I'm sure I qualify because I ran through flaming buildings for two videos last year. And, because I've had a lot of experience with special effects and didn't need a lot of rehearsal time, I helped them meet their production deadline. Why don't we get together to discuss this either Tuesday or Thursday?"

A. Ask for a meeting. You want a *face-to-face meeting. Ask* for it. *And be prepared to ask again.*

In Chapter 15, you'll learn several additional ways to ask for things, but you already know a terrific way: a *choice* of options. It's simply a choice between one thing and another—either one of which is acceptable to you. That's so much better than asking: Will you meet me? When you ask the question that way, you have a 50-50 chance that the answer would be "no."

You want to maximize the chance of hearing "yes," so if you're asking for a meeting, offer choices like two different days or times or places:

"Would you like to meet on Monday or is Wednesday a better day for you?"

"Which is more convenient, morning or afternoon?"

"Should we meet for breakfast at Ptomaine Tommy's or Bertha Beansprouts'?"

B. Build Belief (in You) with Your Best Benefit (for Her). *How could you possibly benefit her and her company?* You will recall that benefits are mostly bottom-line oriented. They help the company make or save money, improve image, reduce or avoid problems, etc.

Remember the mini-stories you wrote? You can use one now. How did your previous employers benefit from your work? Obviously, you'll want to highlight your achievement that relates most closely to the business and the individual you're calling.

More experienced people might have examples like these:

◆ Reduced hours required for annual finished goods inventory by 25% through comprehensive preplanning.

◆ Reduced the vault and mail room force by 47% over 2 years resulting in more than $300,000 savings per year.

◆ Negotiated contracts worth in excess of $1 million to provide traffic reports to 18 radio and TV stations.

◆ Revised monthly close resulting in significant increase in overall accuracy and 30% savings in time.

Highlight your best asset. If you've worked for their major competitor, that alone could make them interested in talking with you.

Your best accomplishment might seem to be unrelated to the kind of work you want to do and the company you're calling. If that's your situation, you'll have to translate your experience into something that's relevant to them.

Example: You managed a fast food outlet part-time to help pay for college. You supervised, scheduled, and trained 15 employees and consistently received outstanding evaluations, in part because of excellent customer satisfaction in your store. Now, you want to persuade Preposterous Promotions, a PR firm, that your fast food experience, plus a 2-year internship at a radio station, qualify you for a job in PR.

"Ms. Dubious: I've had 2 years of PR and promotions experience with station WHAT. My bosses there and at Bitty Burgers, where I managed one of the stores, gave me excellent evaluations because I'm a dedicated employee who meets deadlines and really cares about our customers. Isn't that the kind of person you want at Preposterous Promotions?"

Belief in yourself: the critical component of building belief. By explaining how you can benefit them, you'll encourage the hiring authority to believe in you. But you won't be able to convince anyone else to believe in you unless you do. Whether you're a Ph.D. anthropologist seeking a research position or a vendor selling tomatoes, you've got to be enthusiastic about what you have to offer or there won't be many buyers. It's been said that most people buy not because they believe, but because the salesperson believes. Your conviction and self-confidence generate trust, acceptance, and confidence in others, whether you're communicating with one person or millions.

"The only thing we have to fear is fear itself," President Roosevelt proclaimed in his 1933 inaugural. Most historians give FDR's uplifting words and obvious self-confidence credit for the immediate and remarkable transformation in the attitudes of millions of Americans, whose despair from the Great Depression began to turn towards a sense of hope.

Why the GRAB Formula Works

It's effective because it focuses on the other person. He is, to himself, the most important person in the world. *If you talk about him, he'll listen.*[5] *Before you talk with a prospective employer—on the phone or in person—prepare to answer the question that is uppermost in his mind before he raises it: "What's in it for me?"*[6]

Understanding that should help you overcome any reluctance to use the phone. You need not "fear that the other person won't want to talk." Or feel as though you're "invading their privacy"—the concerns expressed by our outplaced friends. Concentrate on his needs. Can you picture a sign on his head flashing:

What's in it for me?
What's in it for me?   What's in it for me?
What's in it for me?

You Can Juggle Elements of GRAB

Your call will include some, if not all, of the elements of GRAB that you can present in various sequences. For example:

> *"Good morning. Ms. Pin. This is Dan Deposit. As VP for sales, you are probably interested in increasing sales while keeping expenses as low as possible. Is that correct?* (Wait for an answer.) *For the past 2 years, I increased Blue Machine ATM sales by almost 16%. Why don't we get together next week to discuss how I might be able to help you? Which day will be better for you, Monday afternoon or Wednesday morning?"*

> *"Good morning, Ms. Pin. My name is Dan Deposit. I just read about your company's new product line and I assume that you'll want to get some new top-notch people on board. For the past 3 years at Blue Machine, I increased sales by more than 12% a year. Are those the kind of results you're looking for? (*Wait for response. If it is positive, continue with) *Good. Could we get together either Thursday morning or Monday afternoon?"*

You may be thinking that there's no way you could do this—call total strangers and tell them how wonderful you are. That's understandable. This is not what they taught you in high school. Or college. You might be more comfortable with a more modest approach.

> *"Good morning, Ms. Pin. I've had extensive experience in selling ATMs for Blue Machine and Black Boxes. I've read about your new virtual banking ATMs and I think I can be helpful to you as you expand your operations. Would it be possible to get together next week, either Thursday or Friday, to talk about how I could help you?"*

If that will get through Ms. Pin's barrier of preoccupation and you can schedule an appointment with her, that's great! Experiment with some different approaches until you find one that works for you. But don't assume you cannot do it. You can.

Cold calling is not easy to do alone. If you know another job hunter, why not pair off when you're both prepared to call so you can support and encourage each other? You could work as a team—one on the phone, the other listening and cheering (silently, of course).

What's the risk? You could feel uncomfortable. How does being unemployed feel? You might not get a job this way. But you might! You know you have to contact as many hiring authorities as possible to get an offer. This is one way to do that. The choice is yours.

ADDITIONAL SUGGESTIONS FOR EFFECTIVE PHONING

1. Keep it short. A 30–60 second conversation is long enough to make an appointment. Brevity is not only the soul of wit. It shows you respect their time, as well as your own.

2. Understate. Don't promise something unless you're *sure* you can deliver. The fastest way to *blow* your credibility is claim you can do something that you can't. It's always better to *UNDER promise and OVER deliver!*

You *know* you saved your previous employer $50,000 last year in computer costs. From what you know about Ms. Pin's company, you *think* you can be helpful, *but you honestly don't* know. The only way to find out is to meet and explore possibilities.

> *"Ms. Pin. I believe I could be helpful to you because in 5 years, I have generated more than $1 million in sales for Blue Machine ATMs. I'd like to explore how we might be able to work together. Could we meet either Monday morning or Wednesday afternoon?"*

3. Be specific—and be able to back up your claim. You saved $50,000, not "a lot of money," and your mini-story describing the problem, the action you took, and the results you achieved proves it.

4. Be knowledgeable. Your research might surprise, even shock them—pleasantly, of course:

> *"Ms. Pin, the* Bottom-Line Daily *and other financial analysts are enthusiastic about your new virtual banking ATMs. I believe I could be helpful to you because I've been a trouble shooter for Megabucks International virtual banking machines for the past three years, so I really know how these things work. I'm interested in getting into marketing now and I'd like to talk with you about how we could work together. Could we meet for breakfast either Tuesday or Thursday morning?"*

5. Avoid being interviewed on the phone (except for long-distance situations). It's wonderful that Ms. Pin is interested in you. You'll have lots to talk about when you meet, but remember that *the purpose of your call is to schedule a meeting. Hiring commitments are not made in initial phone conversations. But applicants are often eliminated* that way.

Why? For the same reasons your resume could screen you **out**. You might begin to sound *over*qualified, *under*qualified, or just *wrong* for them on the phone. So wrap up your conversation with something like:

"I'm so glad we seem to have so many mutual interests and I'm really looking forward to meeting you. When would it be convenient for you to meet—Monday or Thursday?"

6. Avoid one-sided conversations. Ask open-ended questions.

7. Listen carefully. Being a good listener can get you the appointment. And the job!

8. Don't try to solve the problem on the phone. That's what the meeting is for.

9. Remember the Job Search Rule #1: Resist the temptation to mail your resume to local employers!

Write Your Script

Some people prefer to use an outline, but you'll probably find that if you write your script and *practice so that it does* not *sound rehearsed*, you'll be most effective. The following formula may be useful.

Sample Phone Script[7]
with the Hiring Authority (HA)

HA: "Hello."
You: "Is this _____?"
HA: "Yes."

1. *Identify yourself and explain why you're calling.*

You: "My name is _____ and I'm calling today to make an appointment with you to discuss a mutually beneficial opportunity."

OR

discuss what I can do for you."

2. *Now use your GRAB.*

"I was able to ___(your best benefit for them)___ by ___(achievement)___."

3. *Now ask for an appointment!*

"I could meet you on _____ or _____. Which day is better for you?"

Now take a piece of paper and write your own script. Modify the suggested script until it's something you're comfortable with and *will use.* Otherwise, it's meaningless.

My Script

Identify yourself:

GRAB:

Greeting:

Referral (if appropriate):

Attract attention to problem/need:

Build belief with your Best Benefit:

Close: Ask for a meeting:

Overview: Plan and Prepare Your Approach

Two chapters of this book focus on planning and it's clear that planning and preparation will help you master the job-finding process. To plan and prepare your approach to the hiring authority:

1. Start with your list of target companies that you know something about, including:

   ◆ Name of hiring authority
   ◆ Basic data about the company (products, etc.)
   ◆ Some information about a possible problem or need

2. Develop and *write* a script that is appropriate for him, his company.
3. In that script, you *GRAB his attention* by focusing on *what's in it for him.*
4. *Tape* it and *listen.* How convincing are you? Would *you* be persuaded to make an appointment? If not:
5. Refine your script.
6. Role-play with a friend, spouse.
7. *Practice* so that you are comfortable. And convincing!

Then do it! Call and get your appointment! And celebrate!

When you have set up a meeting with a decision maker, celebrate! You have accomplished the first of two essential steps in finding employment. That's terrific! Reward yourself and savor your success.

Now, let's prepare for step two—persuading decision makers to offer you a job. It could be a smooth ride, but you may encounter some road-blocks. To help insure your success, you'll want to know how to deal with these obstacles. That's the subject of the next chapter.

EMPLOYMENT INSURANCE CHECKLIST

✓ Are you starting with your list of target companies that you know something about?

✓ Are you developing and *writing* a script that is appropriate for him and his company?

✓ Did you tape it and listen?

✓ Are you convincing? If not:

✓ Did you refine your script?

✓ Did you role-play with a friend, spouse?

✓ Did you practice so that you are comfortable and convincing?

✓ Did you call and make an appointment with at least one hiring authority?

CHAPTER 13

❖

How Can You Overcome Objections?

In the process of setting up an appointment with a potential employer, you're practicing the skills of persuasive communications. Preparation plays a key role in that process. Before you call a potential employer for an appointment, for example, you want to be quite sure that you'll be successful. You may get a wonderful response: "Sure, I'd love to see you. Why don't you come over at 3:00 so we'll have plenty of time to talk."

But what if you hear: "I'm too busy . . . Business is terrible . . . Send me a resume . . . This is a bad time . . . We're downsizing here . . . Let me think about it . . . Can you call me next month?"

If you're not prepared, you're apt to hang up. And give up. That doesn't get you where you want to be—inside his office. But if you recognize these statements as objections and respond appropriately, you'll meet many more decision makers. And find your job much sooner.

Anyone can be persuasive if you're both in total agreement at the outset. The skill in persuasive communications—in finding a job or anything else—is convincing the other person when there's some difference of opinion. That's a skill you can learn. And the suggestions offered here will help you do that.

WHAT'S AN OBJECTION?

An objection is a thought which makes the other person hesitate to do what you would like. Most of us are so inundated with requests that we are conditioned to say "no" without really thinking.

Most job seekers assume "no" is a rejection. But you can reframe it, take a *good* look at it, and perceive it as an opportunity to explain what you can do for them. When you have prepared and practiced, you may actually welcome objections, knowing that they are, in fact, steps toward success.

When the other person says he's "not interested" or is "too busy," is he saying: "No, I will not meet you!"? Or is he simply saying: "I'm not convinced that I should take my valuable time for this meeting. You must tell me more. Persuade me!" When you think about it, the definition of an objection is clear. *An objection is a request for more information.*

YOU CAN OVERCOME OBJECTIONS

Start with a Positive Attitude

How you speak, we've pointed out, is even more important than what you say. That's particularly true in dealing with objections. Your manner must be friendly, respectful, and positive. As you respond to an objection, you may disagree, but you must *never* be disagreeable. Or argumentative. That would end the game. And you would lose.

Use a Proven Method

In addition to your positive, friendly manner, use these five steps:[1]

1. Clarify
2. Prepare your answer
3. Answer
4. Stress a benefit of your service
5. Close

1. Clarify. That's the critical first step. Because we live in a world of misunderstandings, it's essential that you're on the same track as the other person. To do that:

- *Listen carefully and respectfully.*
- *Clarify* even when you think you understand. How?
    - Restate the objection as a statement or question. Restating also gives you a little breathing time, and helps you determine how serious this objection really is.

◆ Ask questions. Probe. Be sure there are no misunderstandings.

Objection: *Business is terrible!*

He: *"Business is terrible."*

You: *"Business is terrible?"*

He: *"Yes, this is the worst season we've had in 10 years."*

2. Prepare for the answer. Before you begin to disagree, find something positive to cushion or soften your response. Acknowledge the objection.

◆ Be empathetic. Tell him that you understand how he might feel: "I'm really sorry that . . ."

◆ Agree with him (if possible). "I can certainly agree that the economy could be better . . ."

◆ Compliment him (only if it is sincere). "That's a good question" or "That's certainly a good point."

3. Answer. He may answer his own objection if you ask a question.

You: *"Am I right in thinking that saving money is more important than ever right now?"*

He: *"Saving money is always important, of course. How could you save me money?"*

Note: Questions are always a sign of interest! Listen for them!

4. Stress benefit. Emphasize how you could benefit him.

You: *"As I mentioned before, by analyzing the situation at the YYY company and recommending a new approach, I saved them $150,000 last year alone. And they're still using that program. I think I could do something like that for you, but I can't know for sure until we have a chance to get together."*

5. Close. Ask for an appointment. Offer a choice between two options, either one of which is acceptable.

You: *"Which day would you prefer, Tuesday or Wednesday?"*

Responding to Other Objections You're Apt to Hear

Objection: We're awfully busy. Call back in a few months!

You: *"I hope that means that business is good, but I'm sorry you're too busy to talk. That's just the reason we should meet. I think I could help*

relieve you of some of that burden. That's what I did at EZ Insurance. By reorganizing their claims processing department, I helped them consolidate claims processing, which resulted in saving almost 27% of their staff time."

"If we could meet for just a few minutes and talk more about your situation, I may be able to help relieve you of some of that overload. Why don't we discuss this over breakfast? Is 7:00 or 7:30 better for you?"

OR

"I'd be happy to call back as you suggest, but I think if we had just a few minutes together this week or next, you'd see how I could begin helping you much sooner. It's possible that I could have made a real contribution by the time you want me to call back."

Objection: You have no XYZ experience!

You: *"Have you ever hired anyone who didn't have XYZ experience? Was it a good or bad experience?* (If negative) *Did that person study, learn, and work really hard to make up for it? That's what I'm prepared to do. And I'm sure that you'll be glad you gave me a chance to prove what I could do for you."*

OR

You: *"That's just why you'll want me on your team! I haven't developed any bad work habits yet. You can train me to do things just the way you want."*

Objection: You have no ZZZ degree or AAA certification!

You: *"Did everyone with the ZZZ degree that you hired really work out well for you?"*

OR

You: *"If I had a ZZZ degree, would you hire me right now?"* (If the answer is yes, you could continue.) *"Since I'm enrolled in a ZZZ course this quarter, don't you think it would be a good idea to hire me now so I could apply what I learn to this job and you'll have the benefit of that training right away?"*

Objection: You're overqualified!

You: *"By overqualified, what do you mean?"*

She: *"You've had 11 years of experience in clinical research, with 3 years as manager of your department. That's much more experience than we need for this position."*

You: *"Having that range of experiences means that I can do more for you than someone with less background, doesn't it? I'm sure there are things I could help you with that someone with less background couldn't do, like help train the staff, if that's something you would want. Most important, of course, is that you and the president will know that this department is well managed, and that will make you look good, won't it?"*

    OR

You: *"Overqualified in what area?"*

She: *"Well, quite frankly, we don't need someone with a Ph.D. in English literature."*

You: *"I can see why you might say that, but it's not a problem, is it?"*

She: *"Well, I'm afraid you'd be bored."*

You: *"I honestly think there are some terrific challenges here and I'm excited about learning how the museum collections are computerized. I'm sure I can make a real contribution to your art in literature program while I'm assisting you with museum administration. My mother always told me that education is never wasted. Don't you agree?"*

Objection: We have no money!

You: *"This is really an ideal time to discuss how I might be able to help you save money. Is it possible that you may be spending more than necessary for your _____ (the services you provide)?"*

    OR

    "Don't you think it would be a good investment for you to get started on the artificial originals project so that when you are ready to market it, all the basic groundwork will have been done?"

Objection: Send me your resume!

Remember Job Search Rule #1? Don't Mail Your Resume to Local Employers! Instead of mailing, you might say:

> *"Tell me. When you make a major purchase like a car, do you rely on product literature alone—or do you like to see what you're buying?"*

(Wait for answer.) *"Then you do want to see what you're getting so you can make the best choice, isn't that right?"* (Wait for answer.) *"It's the person, not the piece of paper, that's important to you, isn't it? You want to be sure that the person really fits into your department. That's the reason I'm calling, to help you make the best choice. Would Wednesday or Friday be better for you?"*

> *"Even if you eliminate me from consideration, we'll both have the satisfaction of knowing the decision was substantive, not based on just a piece of paper. Can you tell me if Thursday's a good day for you or would Friday be better?"*

OR

You: *"Haven't you found that a lot of resumes exaggerate? Don't you want to know if I can do something for you and your company? My resume really can't do that. But I can!"*

Objection: We have no openings! OR We're not hiring!

There are more assertive ways of responding to this objection, but most job seekers are not comfortable with them and don't use them. The following response is one that almost anyone can modify and adopt.

You: *"I understand that you have no openings right now. But why don't we get together for a few minutes anyway to see if there might be some task or project that I could help you with. Would Thursday afternoon or Friday morning be more convenient for you?"*

Objection: You have to go through human resources!

You: *"I'd be happy to see your HR people, but I wonder if they know exactly what plans and ideas are in your head. Wouldn't it be better if we met first and talked more about the project to see if we think along the same lines? Then, if we're both still interested, I could see your HR people also. Would Monday afternoon or Tuesday morning be better for you?"*

OR

You: *"I'm sure you've provided HR with all your requirements for the position. But don't you find that it's very hard for someone else to know just who will fit best on your team? That's something you would probably know in just a few minutes. Why don't we get together briefly on Monday or Thursday afternoon?"*

Despite your valiant efforts, it's not always possible to avoid the human resources department. If you cannot circumvent them, use your visit to get as much information as possible.

COMPENSATING ASSETS

No One's Perfect

You may not have the specific degree or particular experience, but you do have compensating assets. Don't assume that the hiring authority will be able to find the "perfect" person.

Being mature and out of the work force for many years are both objections facing many women who have opted for full-time motherhood. When they return to the labor market, they may also face new requirements for the very same job that they had done well in the past.

That was Suzanne's experience. She had worked as a rehabilitation counselor before she took 10 1/2 years to raise her children. When she applied for the same kind of position in 1990, she was confronted with a new hurdle.

"Most companies wanted CRC (certified rehabilitation counselor) after your name. Since I didn't have that, I was eliminated from consideration for the same kind of work I had done years ago."

Fortunately, Suzanne was able to convince her current employer that her experience, discipline, and self-motivation more than compensated for not having the CRC certification.

Turn "Negatives" into Positives

Judy was another mother who returned to full-time employment. She took 14 years off to raise her children, earn her MBA, and decide on a career change (from sales and marketing in the telecommunications field to finance). When she applied for a position at a major bank, she confronted the age issue head on.

"Obviously, I'm more mature than some of my peers here and that's good. I've raised three children and my family is complete, so I won't be taking

pregnancy leaves. I've organized our household efficiently and know the difference between serious problems which need attention right away and less important things which can wait. I just completed my MBA, which means that my education is current and you won't have to pay for it. Now I can devote myself to this job."

After she was hired, Judy asked her boss if her age had been a concern. He conceded that they had wondered about it, but because she approached it so positively, it became a non-issue.

By tackling the objection at the outset, you can neutralize it. Follow Judy's example and turn all the facts about you into benefits for them—and you'll get the job too!

WHEN CAN YOU OVERCOME OBJECTIONS?[2]

Stop worrying that they'll discover your "weakness." Prepare. Then relax. You can often decide when, if ever, to deal with the objection:

◆ Before it comes up
◆ Now
◆ Later
◆ Never

Before. If you keep hearing (or sensing) the same objection again and again, you might start with it and get it out of the way. For example, if you have little work experience or think you look too young or too old:

"Mr. Wonderbread, we've talked on the phone. But this is our first meeting. You may be thinking that I look too young to take on the kinds of responsibilities you've listed in your ad. After we've some time to talk and you know more about what I accomplished at the Lumpy Mattress Company, I think you'll agree that I'm the right person for this job."

If you're at the other end of the age spectrum, you could start with Judy's approach or:

"You can see, Ms. Rye, that I'm over 29. Fortunately, I enjoy excellent health and I keep very fit by (swimming . . . jogging . . . aerobics—whatever you actually do). In fact, I didn't lose a day of work because of illness during my 14 years with Lumpy.

"As I understand it, you need someone in this position who can manage conflicts. I'm sure you want a mature person you can rely on to do that well, isn't that right? When I became general manager for Lumpy, I was able to

resolve several long-standing disputes and negotiate settlements that saved us $90-$100,000 a year. That's the kind of person you're looking for, isn't it?"

Now. *"Although I wasn't able to complete my college requirements before I started at Lumpy, I've enrolled in two evening courses this semester. So I'll be able to work full-time and get my degree by next June. That satisfies your educational requirements, doesn't it?"*

You can offset some objections, like lack of education and experience, by engaging in that activity right now. If your computer skills are not quite up-to-date, you can remedy that by taking some courses. No experience writing press releases? You can do that as a volunteer for a nonprofit organization.

Later. You may want to postpone your answer until you get more information. For example: "I'll be glad to explain that (the lack of degree or the "spotty" work history) in one moment, but first, may I go ahead with this thought about the software you are using?"

Never. Although you must be very careful not to offend the prospective employer, you might not "hear" the problem and just keep emphasizing how you will benefit them. The objection may never be raised again.

KEEP DIGGING

What Is the REAL Objection?[3]

Most of us don't like to hurt other people's feelings (or get sued), so we mask our thoughts with vague, general expressions. "You're overqualified," for example, is often a euphemism for:

You're too old—or
You'll cost too much—or
You're a threat to me, etc.

Ben, a 60-year-old lawyer who was outplaced from a major corporation, was "overqualified" when he applied for a position with a smaller firm. They wanted his expertise but not the high salary and increased health care premiums they assumed his employment would cost. Once he discovered what they really meant by "overqualified," he not only eliminated the objection, he demonstrated his negotiating savvy:

> *"I know I have a lot to offer you with my expertise in international trade, and I want to remain active and productive. Is cost the only reason you're not offering me the position?* (He waited for their affirmative answer.) *Let me explain that I've done an assets/liabilities balance sheet and I know what I need to earn. You won't have to provide any benefits at all because those are taken care of. Why don't we quickly settle on a figure that'll be fair for both of us so I can get to work on a new international business development plan for you?"*

Older employees may be more willing to realize that the company needs them for the short term—one or two years—and doesn't want to—or can't—make a long-term commitment. Their lower expectations may make it easier for the company to hire them as "Ms. Fix It" for short-term assignments.

Why Don't They Want to Meet You?

When decision makers protest that they're "too busy," they're really saying that you haven't convinced them that the benefits of seeing you outweigh the costs (their time or money—which are, essentially, the same). You'll be more persuasive if you describe the meeting in terms of a:

- ◆ good investment of their time (rather than a cost)
- ◆ small sample—limited to a few minutes.

After you've persuaded them to meet you, you can use the same techniques to convince them to hire you. That is, you represent a good investment (of their money, as well as time). You can also make it easier for them to buy your services by making them available on a trial or interim basis. After all, all new employment, regardless of how "permanent," is, essentially, probationary anyway.

If they still insist that they don't need any _____ services (whatever it is you provide), the reason could be:

1. You don't know enough about their needs or they don't know enough about how you can help them, which means that you

could still persuade them. For example, they may think they don't
need additional services until they realize that your service is:

◆ better

◆ faster

◆ has some other added value

2. It's a valid objection. You really cannot help them, so you should
go on to the next opportunity.

Key Thing to Remember in Dealing with Objections

If you recall only one thing from this chapter, remember to *clarify—and not
simply accept—roadblocks* that are thrown in your path. The easiest way to
clarify is simply to repeat what they said as a question. "I'm overqualified?
. . . You're too busy? . . . You're downsizing?" (In fact, many companies that
are downsizing are simultaneously hiring.)

Repeating the objection will give you a little breathing room—time to
think—so you can respond appropriately. When you do this diplomati-
cally, with a smile, you'll win their respect. And possibly the job. Shrink-
ing violets won't survive self-employment, even in the floral business. But
you will survive—and thrive—because you know that what you have to
offer will really benefit your next employer. And you really want to give
them that opportunity.

TELEPHONE PRESENTATION: REVIEW

You can greatly improve your employment insurance coverage by using
the techniques outlined in Chapters 10 through 13. After you target your
market and get past the gatekeeper, you're ready to approach the decision
maker. Because you're well prepared, you'll have a positive attitude and
feel confident that he'll meet you. The major steps in that conversation
are:

1. Identify yourself
2. GRAB his attention by:
   Greeting
   Referral
   Attract attention to his need and a possible solution
   Ask for meeting
   Build belief in yourself with your Best Benefit for them

3. Overcome objections
   Clarify
   Prepare for answer
   Answer
   Stress benefit
   Close
4. Close: Ask for and schedule a meeting

We've quoted some outplaced executives who remained unemployed for an unnecessarily long time because they didn't know how to manage the whole telephoning process. Now you do. Make the telephone your friend by using it every day to make appointments with decision makers, either by referral or calling "cold." All it takes is preparation and practice. What other skill can you acquire quickly that will produce such dramatic results?

You've learned to overcome many of the objections that decision makers might express when you call. And you've persuaded one of them to meet you. Your next step, the meeting!

EMPLOYMENT INSURANCE CHECKLIST

✓ What will you say if the hiring authority you call claims she's "too busy . . . we're downsizing," etc.?
✓ Do you have a positive attitude?
✓ Is your manner friendly and respectful?
✓ Can you clarify?
>   prepare an answer?
>
>   answer?
>
>   stress a benefit?
>
>   close?

✓ What are your compensating assets?
✓ Can you turn "negatives" into positives?
✓ Regardless of the outcome, can you remain polite, positive, and empathetic?

CHAPTER 14

❖

The Meeting

You've done it! You've scheduled a meeting with a hiring authority next Tuesday at 9:00 a.m.! There are only four days to get ready. What do you do?

FIRST, PUT THE INTERVIEW IN PERSPECTIVE

Too many job seekers perceive this meeting as a kind of target practice in which *they're* the target. Just thinking about it gives them sweaty palms. After all, employers hold all the cards, don't they?

Not at all. This meeting is an exchange of information between you and them. It's a dialogue, a conversation between equals. If you happen to be unemployed right now, don't let that diminish you in any way. There's no longer any stigma to being unemployed. So many good people have been restructured out of their jobs that it's almost a badge of honor.

Their Perspective

The decision maker, like everyone else, wants to know what's in it for him. And his organization. Hiring decisions are among the most important judgments a manager makes and they're never easy. He's trying to figure you out why you're applying for this job. Are you too young? Too old? Will you fit in with the others? Are you independent enough, or would you have to be directed all the time? Lots of questions. And risk! If he makes a poor choice, he not only has an inadequate employee to deal with. But his own career suffers because he's evaluated on his ability to make good decisions. Mistakes are costly financially and emotionally. For everyone.

Even in a buyer's market, the employer doesn't hold all the cards. First of all, most hiring authorities are not good interviewers. Very few have been trained in interviewing techniques. Once you've read this book, planned, prepared, and practiced for your meeting, you'll probably be better equipped than they are. Just knowing that should give you an advantage.

Your Perspective

Your purpose at this meeting is clear. A job *offer.*[1] Not necessarily a job. That's your ultimate goal, of course. But your *immediate* objective is an offer. When you have several offers, you're in an enviable position. You have choices. There are several other benefits also:

- It will make you feel good. Someone wants you!
- You will be able to tell others about your offer. That's not only a confidence booster, but could give you some leverage with another employer. (The fact that someone else wants you makes you a more desirable candidate to others.)
- You may be weary of looking and decide that something is better than nothing right now.
- You may be able to sweeten the deal, negotiate better compensation, etc. (See Chapter 17.)
- This is an excellent opportunity to practice asking for the job. Take advantage of it, even if you are not totally thrilled with this opportunity.

How can you ask for a job that you're not excited about? Think about the above. You want to be able to *consider* this opportunity, don't you? Give yourself as many options as possible by asking for them. It may turn out to be a better deal than you had thought originally.

Your secondary purpose: Make them glad they met you. Focus on them, their needs and their primary buying motive. Most companies don't hire on the basis of one meeting. It usually takes two or three. Be sure you're invited back.

You are most persuasive when you say: I know I can do the job because I've done it before and I've done it well.[2] If that's not the case, stress your compensating assets and your potential. By being interested and enthusiastic, focusing on them and communicating that you're results oriented, capable, flexible, trustworthy, and trainable, you'll create enough interest so that they'll want to see you again.

What do you think of them? Your visit to their office is, of course, a chance to assess them—the organization, its culture, the people you'd be working with, as well as the job and the opportunity it represents. What are your impressions? What do you see and hear that make you enthusiastic? Or wary? If you're a button-down type, do you think you would be happy in a rather chaotic atmosphere?

Every organization has a certain style and it's important for you to determine how well you would fit in. If you think this culture is perfect for you, tell them. That will help all of you feel comfortable with each other.

PREPARATION: KEY TO YOUR SUCCESS

Being prepared about the company, the hiring authority, etc., as well as about yourself will give you the confidence you need to convince them to make you an offer.

More Preparation about Yourself

Review the reasons why they should hire you. Since you know what you can offer and can communicate that well, you'll need only a brief review of your worksheets, accomplishments, and mini-stories. Review your list of the five most attractive things about you from an employer's perspective. Do they fit this employer? Are these good reasons why they should hire you? If not, revise your list.

Get Ready for the Q & A

Make a list of questions they will probably ask. Then answer them.

The basic answering rule: Write out short, factual answers.[3] Answer honestly in terms of the job to be filled and your relevant experience, accomplishments and the benefits you would bring. Don't apologize. Rehearse, role-play, and revise your answers until you feel comfortable.

By doing that, you'll gain control and avoid tell-tale physical reactions like blushing and squirming.

Four Categories of Questions

Be prepared to answer questions about:[4]

1. your background
2. your personality
3. your motivation
4. your salary requirements.

1. Your background: The hiring authority may open with a question like, "Tell me about yourself."

Your response: Review your recent past (no more than 10 to 15 years) in an organized, interesting way. Prepare a 2-minute summary of your work experience, education, and, if relevant, community activities. Be yourself—honest and sincere. Don't try to fake knowledge. Emphasize what you think will interest them.

Talk in terms of your achievements. Use mini-stories and avoid overly detailed presentations. Whet their appetites instead.

2. Your personality: What kind of manager are you?

Your response: Try to find out about their management style, corporate culture, etc. Then respond appropriately.

3. Your motivation: What is the ideal job for you? What did you like most about your last job? Least? What are your strengths? Weaknesses?

Your response: Emphasize challenge, growth, leadership opportunities, etc. Be specific. Mini-stories could be appropriate here.

4. Your salary requirements:

Salary Rule: DO NOT discuss compensation until you have a *firm* job offer.

Any discussion of compensation at this stage is premature. Potential employers want to know what your salary expectations are so they can decide whether or not to consider you. If you're not in their ball park (too high or too low), they'll eliminate you. Before you have a firm job offer, explain that salary is not your major consideration and that you need to know more about the position before discussing compensation: "It's really the opportunity, not the salary, that's most important to me." Then ask a question about the job.

Whenever you're asked to indicate salary requirements, on an application, for example, just write "negotiable." (For more about salaries and negotiations, see Chapter 17.)

What about Tough Questions?

Tough questions are the ones you wish they wouldn't ask. They usually deal with your reasons for leaving your last job and your past job performance.

Handling tough questions is, in some respects, like overcoming objections. They may even be the same issues. One difference, however, is that after you have answered an objection, you ask for a decision. After you've answered a tough question, you'll want to change the subject.

Your strategy for answering tough questions is to answer them briefly and honestly. Then, *immediately change the subject*. One way to do that is to ask a question about the job, the organization, their plans, etc. Rehearse that as part of your answer. You can mash tough questions into whipped cream if you:

Anticipate the question.

Prepare by writing a brief, factual answer ahead of time.

Ask a question to change the subject after you have answered the inquiry.

Practice. Role-play, tape, and revise.

Examples:

Hiring Authority (HA): Why were you let go?

Your response: Be positive, with no hint of hostility toward your former employer. In general, avoid discussing personalities. (If you've followed our suggestions, you have already contacted your previous boss and asked what you can honestly say about your termination. Make sure they will back up your explanation.)

Example: It was a corporate decision over which I had no control.

OR: Our whole department was eliminated.

OR: The top two people from each department were eliminated and I was the second in command.

OR: After the merger, it became clear that the new owners had a different management philosophy.

HA: Why have you been out of work so long?

Your response: I've had some offers that I turned down because I wasn't that confident about the product/service. I know I have to be enthusiastic about what I represent. And that's the way I feel about your company. Now, I'm really interested in what you said earlier about _____. Could you please explain _____?

OR

I saw no growth opportunity in that company and made the mistake of leaving before I lined up another job. An article in last month's *Virtual Reality* about new developments in the industry indicated that some companies are getting into virtual vacation packages. Can you tell me if you are planning _____?

HA: You've had 3 jobs in the past 4 years. Why so much change?

Your response: I didn't have the authority I needed to do a really effective job at Puffed-up Pastries. I gave it my best shot and tried to remedy the situation, but nothing really changed. So after 11 months, I left. Prior to that, I was the most recent hire at Have Your Cake and Eat It. When business turned sour, I was laid off. Mr. Torte said he was really sorry to let me go. He was the one who suggested that I call you. I'm really interested in knowing how you managed to do _____?

OR

My job was not what I thought it would be at Puffed-up Pastries. Frankly, I didn't feel my work there was very meaningful, and I know I can do much more. I tried to take on some additional responsibilities, but that didn't seem to be working out the way I had hoped. Tell me, have you ever considered _____?

HA: Where will you be 5 years from now?

Your response: I'll want to be in a position where I have an opportunity to learn and grow and take on greater responsibilities. From what I've seen here, you would offer that kind of challenge.

Can you be "overprepared"? Some people caution against too much preparation. Naturally, you don't want your answers to sound "canned." But when you watch a world-class gymnast or skater, do you think their seemingly effortless movements come from being overprepared? Or have they practiced so well that it only *looks* easy?

More Preparation about Them

Spend most of your pre-meeting time learning about them—the company, their competitors, the hiring authority, etc. Read every pertinent thing you can get hold of and talk with as many relevant people as possible to get the latest information.

Before you make any commitment to an organization, you'll want to know how solid it is. If you have a broker, call and ask for a financial report on the company. You can also get financial analysts' reports in *Corporate Industry Research Reports*, available on microfiche or CD-ROM at some major libraries. You may recall that other resources for financial information about corporations were described in Chapter 6.

Don't go to an interview unless you have at least the "basics" about the organization, their products, etc. For example:[5]

- ◆ Is it privately held?
- ◆ Parent company or division?
- ◆ How many years has it been in business?
- ◆ What is their anticipated growth and direction in the next 5 years?

- Who are their major competitors?
- What are their major products?
- What is their major market(s)?

Other questions that could be explored in advance:

- Who is the hiring authority and what does he need, want?
- What problem can I help them solve?
- How could I help solve it?
- What does this position lead to?
- Is there a training program? Where? How long?
- How urgently do they need someone?
- How many interviews can I expect?
- What is their time frame for the hiring process?
- Is he the sole decision maker? If not:
- Who else is involved in hiring process?
- Where are additional interviews, if any, held?
- Are there tests? If so, what kind? When?

In preparing for your meeting, "be creative," suggests Anne, a customer service manager for a major health insurer. "Do something that sets you apart, that makes you memorable. Not something that's totally bizarre, of course. Just coming in with questions sets you apart from the rest." From your research, you should be able to develop a list of 20 to 30 questions (like some of the above) to ask at your meeting.

THE "NUTS AND BOLTS" OF INTERVIEWING

Prepare to Make a Good First Impression

Avoid last-minute hassles by making sure that you have suitable clothing in good condition. The general rule: Dress one level above what people in that position would wear to work. When in doubt, err on the side of caution. A conservative suit is appropriate for almost all situations.

Your good physical appearance is important because how you look represents the tip of the proverbial iceberg. They can't see the really important things—your competence, industriousness, resilience, dedication to excellence, etc. When substantive information is lacking, trivial things, like a missing button or sloppy shoes, gain significance. So watch the details and look as good as you can. At a minimum, be sure that your clothing and grooming are *not a distraction* in any way.

Get detailed information regarding the location before your meeting. Trace the route on your map, if you're not familiar with the location, and allow plenty of time for traffic jams, bad weather, etc.

In your attache case, take:

- ◆ Name of person, address, directions, and phone number (in case you're detained and must call)
- ◆ Your questions, a notepad, and a pen
- ◆ Your calendar (to schedule a follow-up appointment, if necessary)
- ◆ Letters of reference from previous employers, clients, and customers. Names, addresses, phone numbers of other references
- ◆ Something to read, like an annual report or something relevant, so that you don't waste your time if you're kept waiting

On Arrival: Some Interviewing Basics

1. Time it right. Plan to get into the office 8 to 10 minutes before your appointment. That will give you time to make some observations, review company materials that may be in the reception area, and relax. (If you arrive much earlier, read in your car or elsewhere in the building. Arriving too early could communicate that you're not very busy. You are. You're engaged in a full-time job-finding mission.) Tardiness, of course, is totally unacceptable. If you are unavoidably detained, call to explain.

2. Look like you belong. Ask where you can hang up your coat, umbrella, etc., so that you look like the others in the office.

3. Project confidence with your good posture and calm demeanor.

4. Be positive, friendly, and polite with everyone in the office. That's not only good manners—the observations of office personnel could affect hiring decisions.

5. Don't smoke, even if you are invited to do so.

6. Communicate alertness through your body language. In the decision maker's office, sit upright, leaning forward slightly.

YOUR MEETING

First Encounter

You have only one chance to make a good first impression. Do it! Exude confidence as you smile and make eye contact, simultaneously extending your hand and shaking hands *firmly*. Maintain eye contact while you introduce yourself and tell Ms. Muffit how glad you are to meet her.

The handshake should be professional—neither a bone crusher nor a bowl of jelly. Keep a handkerchief ready for a last-minute wipe if you're apt to perspire.

Some people who find it hard to make eye contact have learned that if they look at the bridge of the other person's nose, they give the impression that they are making eye contact.[6] A trivial thing, like your inability to look people in the eye, could be interpreted as a sign of dishonesty. That alone might disqualify you from the job! Don't let that happen. If these incidental things are difficult for you, practice until you get them right.

You may have persuaded Ms. Muffit to hire you already! It's been estimated that most hiring decisions are made in the first 15 seconds. Hiring decisions, like other buying decisions, are often made emotionally, then backed up with logic.

Get and Hold Their Attention

You may have used the GRAB formula to get this appointment and it's appropriate again.

Greet her by name, as you've already done, and use her name from time to time. Get on a first-name basis as quickly as possible unless you feel uncomfortable doing that. You can initiate the use of first names by saying: "Everyone calls me Vicki" or "Please call me Hal."

Refer to your mutual friend or acquaintance, if appropriate. Another way to break the ice is to pay a compliment, *if you can do so sincerely*. A favorable comment about the office (space, decor, view) or how helpful her secretary was in providing directions would be appropriate.

Be observant. Asking about an unusual picture, paperweight, or another object may prompt her to talk about something pleasurable. A mutual interest is perfect bonding material. People hire people who are like them.

When Sandy applied for her job as the director of public information for a not-for-profit planning agency, she and her future boss hardly talked about public relations. Sandy's appreciation for a small, exotic Indian sculpture in the executive's office started an animated conversation about traveling, which both women thoroughly enjoyed. Sandy was well qualified for the position. And because they had so much in common, she had an insurmountable edge over the other applicants. "We hit it off so well," Sandy remarked. "I just knew I had the job!"

The rest of the GRAB formula, as you know, is:

Ask questions to learn more about their needs. **A**ttract attention to your services that may help meet their needs. **B**uild belief in your services with your **B**est **B**enefit for them.

Some Communications Basics

The #1 rule in communications: People prefer talking to listening. Knowing that gives you an important advantage. For some of us "born talkers," it means biting our tongues. But it's worth it.

Bill was discouraged after his first meeting with Leonard, the hiring authority. "He kept talking," Bill complained. "I hardly had a chance to sell myself." What Bill didn't recognize was that the interview went very well. Leonard's monologue meant that he was very comfortable with Bill and wanted to share information with him. Bill had already "sold" himself without either one of them realizing it—the best of all possible worlds.

The #2 rule in communications: If you're talking, you're not learning. Your ability to persuade depends heavily on your skill in getting information, especially from the decision maker. So although this meeting is an exchange of information, you don't really want an *even* exchange. You'll benefit most by making it a lopsided conversation.

Encourage them to talk 70% of the time, which leaves you with only 30%. It's a useful ratio to remember, especially if you tend to be a "talker." But let your good judgment prevail in applying this formula. Your mission is to get a job offer. To do that, you'll have to satisfy their need to know about you by answering their questions fully and to convince them that the benefits of hiring you outweigh the costs. The 70:30 formula is only a guideline to help you accomplish your objective.

Ask Questions Skillfully

The questioning skill is not just asking questions, but getting the information you need. It's essential, however, that you make them feel comfortable with you. This is a conversation, not an interrogation, and you'll want to maintain a consultative, genial atmosphere. Be sensitive to how you're coming across and back off if necessary.

1. First, you must decide what you want to know.
2. Then, request permission to ask questions and take notes. "You don't mind if I ask a few questions, do you? And I want to be sure I remember what you say, so I'll take some notes, if that's all right with you."

   Taking a few notes at significant meetings like this is a good idea, as long as it doesn't disrupt the flow of the conversation. He will probably be impressed that you prepared some questions in advance and are interested enough in what he's saying to want to take notes.
3. Start with broader topics and then focus your questions more narrowly.
4. Ask open-ended questions, like how, what, where, who, and when?
5. Listen with all your senses, being especially observant of their body language. What was said and what was *not* said? Good listening means that you listen carefully and actively to their answers. It's trying to understand the other person's point of view, paying attention not only to the *words* of the speaker but also the *feelings* they convey. A good listener puts himself in the other person's shoes.

   Watch and listen to their body language and speech and try to reflect that. If the other person speaks quickly—or hesitantly—do the same. You'll find that *the more you are like them, the more comfortable they are with you.* And that comfort level gets translated into job offers.
6. Don't interrupt.
7. Build on previous responses. Did you get the information you need? What is the gap between what they have and what they want?

8. Find out which benefits he wants, what's really important to him and *why* he wants it. In general, he'll buy what appears to promise the greatest number of benefits, but you must be careful not to assume too much.

   A hospital administrator, for example, was explaining to a prospective employer how she had helped her former employer save money. Avoiding a loss, she knew, is usually a more powerful accomplishment than making a gain. Her achievements were impressive and she was justly proud of them. But saving money was *not* this decision maker's primary interest. His major concern was expanding market share.

You're like a doctor diagnosing a patient. Your mission is to find out where it hurts. Then you can suggest a remedy. But you don't want to say, "You have a problem," or appear to tell them how to run their business. It's preferable to say something like: "From what I can tell, it looks like there's a situation here that I think I can help with" and emphasize the benefits you would bring.

Asking Questions When There Is a Specific Job Opening

When there is a specific job opening, several kinds of questions are appropriate,[7] including:

Interest questions. These show your interest in the company, position, and products/services, as well as the people, including peers, subordinates, and superiors. You might ask the decision maker how he got into this field and progressed to his current position.

Job satisfaction questions focus on the job, such as:

- What are the company's top priorities?
- What would your major responsibilities be?
- What authority would you have to carry them out?
- Who would you be interacting with?
- What is a typical day like?
- What is an atypical day like?

Past performance questions could explore issues like:

- Who held the job previously and what happened to them?
- What kind of performance do they expect?
- What kind of education and experience do they look for?
- How would they describe their ideal candidate?

If There Is No Specific Job Opening

Without a specific job opening to focus on, your approach is more entrepreneurial. The decision makers may not know what they want. Or they may have put some problems on the back burner because they didn't know of a solution. You might ask questions like:

- What are the biggest headaches you have in (this area)?
- What are your plans for the future?
- What have you tried to remedy this situation?
- How long has this situation existed?
- What parts of the organization are affected by this situation?

Then, you can develop a proposal to address their needs.

EMPHASIZE BENEFITS

For Them

Can you help them make money, save money, avoid or reduce hassles, pain, and suffering? Many of these are bottom-line benefits, but people are often hired for more personal reasons. They convince the prospective employer that they'll make him look good. That's what Michelle did.

Tom's hard work and diligence had paid off. His new assignment put him in charge of a whole department. Tall and athletic, he appeared confident. But inside, he was desperate. Tom had no idea how to get his department moving and fulfill top management's high expectations of him.

His only hope was to find someone who could bail him out. He prayed for an angel to fill the newly created position of marketing manager. Michelle did not look like an angel and had little formal marketing experience. But she was bright and understood marketing instinctively. At their meeting, she emphasized her creativity, energy, and contacts. Her trump card: "I'm sure we would work well together. And *I'll make you look good.*" She did. And they both flourished.

Not for You

Your personal needs—for security, for a job, for this one because it's conveniently located or because it pays well—must be kept out of the interview. They're not relevant. Other needs, like your need to be contributing, working in a stimulating environment, helping others who are less fortunate, being part of this wonderful enterprise, can help you persuade them in this meeting because such needs are job related. So is the fact that you're a hard worker, a good contributor to team efforts, flexible, eager to learn and be challenged. Your focus is always on the hiring authority and the company.

Universal Hiring Rule: The employer will hire if the benefits of hiring outweigh the costs.

That seems like a straightforward cost/benefit analysis. The costs of hiring you are quantifiable: your salary and benefits. But how can the benefits you bring to the employer be measured? They are, at best, only projections of your past experience. That's why being able to demonstrate your ability to make money and save money for previous employers is so important. If you can show that you saved or generated more money than you cost, hiring you is an excellent investment for your next employer. That's all very logical.

But hiring decisions, we have pointed out, are emotional as well as logical. It's been estimated that 75% of the hiring decision is based on personality traits and communication; 25% on work history.

Compensate with Commitment

Radiate enthusiasm! Don't underestimate what passion and commitment can do to compensate for what you might lack in credentials. Judy, the financial analyst we met in the last chapter, who has recently been on both sides of the desk, observes:

> *"The interviewing process is very intimidating. But people on the other side of the desk are really eager for you to sell yourself. They're looking for someone who is enthusiastic, who believes he or she can do it and wants to do it."*

Find Out Where You Stand

Your meeting with a hiring authority is an accomplishment. It's one of the two essential steps in the hiring process. The second step—persuading them to offer you a job—requires understanding and preparation. You have done a very good job of persuading so far. You know what you are selling and who needs it; you have reached them and gotten their attention. In the process, you have gained knowledge about yourself and about them, what they need and want. You have overcome their objections and emphasized the benefits you can bring. Now it's time to wrap this up. In the next chapter, we'll outline some ways you can do that.

EMPLOYMENT INSURANCE CHECKLIST

- ✓ Do you know why they should hire you?
- ✓ Are you aware that your objective is a job offer, not necessarily a job?
- ✓ Are you making them glad they met you?
- ✓ Did you review your accomplishments and responsibilities, as well as reasons why they should hire you?
- ✓ Can you answer the questions they'll probably ask?
- ✓ Have you written your answers to tough questions?
- ✓ Have you done additional research about the organization?
- ✓ Do you have a list of questions you can ask them?
- ✓ Is your clothing in good shape for this meeting?
- ✓ Do you know exactly where the meeting place is?
- ✓ Are you asking questions in a pleasant, consultative manner?
- ✓ Have you practiced your listening skills?
- ✓ Are you listening 70% of the time?
- ✓ Are you calm, poised, and enthusiastic?

CHAPTER 15

❖

Wrapping Up Your Meeting

TAKE THE INITIATIVE

Most job seekers allow their meetings to end ambiguously, with vague statements like: "We'll be in touch." No one is sure what that means. You can do better.

Thank them very much for the meeting and express interest and enthusiasm for working with them. For example: "I'm really interested in this opportunity and know I could do a good job for you." Or, "I'm sure I would be a real asset to you and your organization. This is just the kind of opportunity I've been looking for." Then, ask if there is any additional information they would like to have. Wait for an answer. Then, at a minimum, find out where you stand and what their next step will be. You can do this in several ways:

1. Ask for a summary
2. Ask what their next step is
3. Ask for the job

1. Ask for a summary. Many job seekers will say something like: "I wonder if you could tell me where we stand at this point?" That's a very mild way of asking for a summary that most people would be comfortable saying. In response, they might give you an idea of how well you impressed them, but you're apt to hear something noncommittal.

Or you take a more assertive approach. You're not cocky. Or cute. But you would like to know what she's thinking.

"Ms. Muffit, it seems to me that you have 3 choices.[1] You could:

- ◆ Hire me right now
- ◆ Dismiss me right now
- ◆ Or consider me further.

"Can you please tell me your decision?" Wait for an answer. "Am I being seriously considered?" OR "If you were sole decision maker, would you offer me the job now?" Wait for an answer. If it's noncommittal, you can say:

"If you're not ready to make me an offer now, and you're not ready to dismiss me, then shouldn't we set up another meeting? Would you like to do that right now, or should I call and schedule our next meeting with your secretary?"

Another version of the summary is to ask where you stand in relation to the other candidates. If you can get that information, it could help you decide whether to go for the gold or think about other options.

You can also summarize your meeting by listing all the positives, such as the benefits you would bring, and ask for confirmation. If you decide to use this approach, be sure your manner is very diplomatic and gentle, so that you're getting little agreements and not sounding the least bit prosecutorial.

"You agree that I could make a significant contribution in the _____ department, don't you? And that I could increase the efficiency of the operation? And that would save you money, isn't that right?"

2. Ask what their next step is. This is really the flip side of asking for a summary. Basically, you want to know where you go from here. It's the most common way for job seekers to end meetings, if they ask for anything at all. You'll also want to get some idea of their time frame so you can follow up effectively.

"Can you tell me what your next step would be? Do you have any idea when you're likely to be making a decision?"

You could keep the initiative by adding,

"You don't mind if I check back with you in a week or so, do you? Which day would you suggest? Is the morning a good time to reach you, or would the afternoon be better for you?"

That might be a good way to end the meeting if you're very unsure of the organization and/or the kind of opportunity you would have there. The company might be so new that you haven't been able to get much information so far and you feel it's definitely premature to ask for the job. You might want to ask for another meeting so that you'll be better able to assess the opportunity.

3. Ask for the job.

CLOSING

It May Be a Necessity[2]

For some employers, your ability to ask for the job is a requirement. Sales managers, for example, insist that applicants ask for the job. Their reasoning is compelling. If the applicant won't ask me for the job, how will he ask the customer for an order? Sales managers are not the only employers who share this view. A geologist with a major oil company is one of many employers who believes: "If they're not interested enough to ask for the job, we're not interested in hiring them!" As an entrepreneur selling your services, you really cannot afford not to get a decision.

The Advantages of Closing

Other hiring authorities may not *expect* you to ask for the job, but doing so is very advantageous. It shows that you're confident and mature enough to handle their decision—good or bad. Your ability to close can easily be decisive in the competitive hiring process. Also, having their decision helps you gain some control and plan ahead. Isn't it better to know where you stand than to go through weeks or months of waiting and hoping?

What Is Closing?

A close (or closing) is simply a request for a decision. It's something you did when you asked for a meeting with a potential employer. And you got it! Now, you want him to buy your services.

The Logic of Closing

Ask and you shall receive. The converse is also true. If you don't ask, you probably won't receive. Children are excellent at getting what they want because they ask. And, sometimes, keep on asking until they get what they want. That can be annoying, of course, so in the process of growing up, we've been trained *not* to ask. We've been socialized to believe that it's somehow impolite to ask for what we want.

So we fantasize. About a white knight whispering in our ear: "You're doing such a magnificent job, we're giving you a $50,000 raise and promoting you to director." Or hiring authorities entreating us: "Your credentials are fabulous and we'd be honored if you'd join us. Would this paneled office with a view of the coast be suitable?"

That *might* happen. But how likely is it? You can help make your fantasy a reality by making it easy for them to buy your services. Not, of course, through childish pleading and whining, but by learning to ask for a decision *professionally*.

Understanding the Emotions of Closing

Asking for something is an emotional event for them, as well as for you. Most people don't like making decisions because there is always some risk. In the hiring process, those risks can be substantial, as you know. To understand what's going on in their minds, think about the last time you bought something—especially a major purchase.

What motivated you to buy?[3] It was probably one of the following:

◆ *Fear of loss and hope of gain*
   Fear of loss can include loss of time, money, safety, property, health, loved ones, possessions. Hope of gain includes the possibility of saving money, meeting personal and financial commitments, gaining time, safety, etc.
◆ *Pleasure and avoidance of pain*
   Pleasure includes comfort, convenience, enjoyment, admiration of others, luxury, good health, sexual attraction, good food, drink, desire to possess, etc.
   Avoidance of pain includes protection, relief of pain, security, safety, good health, and less worry.
◆ *Pride and desire for approval*
   Pride includes acceptance, self-improvement, social acceptance, affection, learning, admiration, prestige, etc.

Your emotions peak when you ask for the job. Your positive attitude and belief in yourself will empower you to ask. You begin by **assuming** they will want your services. That in itself is a close: the **assumptive close**.

But there is, of course, the possibility of rejection. And failure. No one likes rejection. But you can learn to **acknowledge your frustration.** If you've been turned down for a job, review and use some of the techniques for dealing with anger outlined in Chapter 2. After you've cooled off, analyze your meeting. Ask yourself: Would I buy my services? If the answer is no, don't ask anyone else! If you don't believe in yourself, who will? Without that basic belief, you cannot be convincing.

TIME AND TIMING

Interest Level and Time

The cliche that timing is everything certainly applies to closing. The diagram on page 192 shows the relationship between time and the employer's level of interest from the moment you contact him through several appointments until the end.[4] You build interest when you contact the employer and persuade him to see you. Then you generate more interest when you explain how you can benefit him. If he can envision himself benefiting from your services, he'll really **want** your services.

Let's imagine that this decision maker has been working nonstop, unable to take a vacation all year. You find out that he's an avid skier and has been yearning for a ski vacation in Norway. Paint the picture of him glissading down pristine slopes, enjoying the magnificent scenery, while you're "minding the store." It's obvious from his wistful look that he's really intrigued with the idea of having you assist him.

But his interest level does not remain high because other demands crowd in on his attention as soon as you leave. It's been estimated that interest level decreases 50% for every 24 hours of time that passes after your contact.

Maintaining interest is like pushing the proverbial boulder up a hill, as you'll probably learn when you follow up. It's exhausting just to keep that

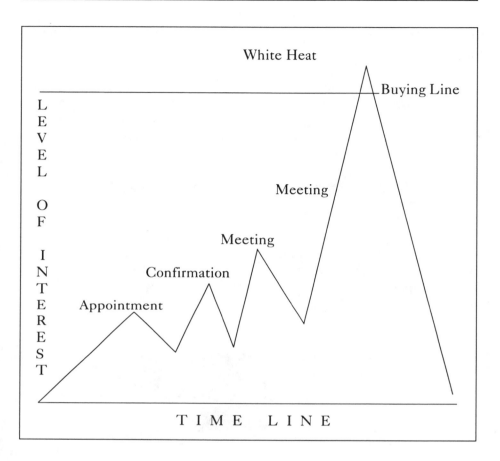

boulder from sliding back. So you have to make the most of each face-to-face opportunity to persuade him that your services will benefit him and his company. Once he's convinced that he really wants your services, he's past the buying line—into the region of white heat. That's when you must get his commitment. After that, his interest falls dramatically, as the chart shows.

How do you know when the other person is past the buying line? You cannot know for sure. Even experts in body language differ in their interpretations of "buying signals." When the decision maker scratches his head or blows his nose—what does he *really mean?* You're on much more solid ground if you keep sounding him out about what he thinks. The word "close" sounds like something you do at the end of your presentation, but waiting until the end means not only lost opportunities but a basic misunderstanding of the whole process of persuasive communications.

Ask for—and get—agreements on key points along the way. By listening carefully and getting confirmation as you go along, your closing question will be simply a culmination or extension of a whole series of understandings. You won't feel like you're pushing and he won't feel pressured because his commitment will flow so naturally from your series of little agreements.

How Often Do You Have to Ask?

Once *may* be enough. But be prepared for more. Don't be put off with your first "no." Or "maybe." Persistence pays. Even though you are assuming that the decision maker will go along with your thinking, be prepared to ask again. That's when knowing several ways to get a commitment will help—not only in getting a job but in getting other agreements as well.

"Ms. Muffit, I know I can do this job because I've done it before and I've done it well. I'm really enthusiastic about working with you and the other people I've met here at Spiderweb Mills. The work you're doing here meshes really well with what I've been doing at Spectacular Silkworms, and I'd love to get started soon. Would you like me to begin in two weeks or would the first of November be better for you?" Then wait for her answer. You may have persuaded her to make you an offer.

More Objections

But you may encounter more roadblocks. To overcome these, be prepared to use the same techniques that worked so well before. You may hear:

Objection: *I need to interview more people!*

Most job seekers would not recognize this as an objection: they would "buy" it. After all, it's not unreasonable for the employer to want to see other candidates before making a decision. At this point, these interviewees might ask the employer when a decision would be made, express their interest, and leave.

Another option is to overcome the objection.

Clarify   **You:** "You need to interview more people?"
                She: "Yes. I don't want to rush this."

Prepare   **You:** "I can certainly appreciate that you want to be careful in making an important decision like this. May I ask you: What are the 3 main attributes you are looking for in a candidate for this job?"
                She: "We're looking for someone with X, Y, and Z."

Answer	**You:** "Yes, I can see why X, Y, and Z would be important here. I'm sorry—apparently I didn't to tell you enough about myself. We've already talked about how I used my X and Z to get very good results at Spectacular Silkworms. Would you agree that my experience clearly shows that I have X and Z?" Wait for an answer. "Good. In fact, my Y ability was probably the reason I was promoted at Fishy Scales. Mr. Perch really appreciated my leadership, especially during the last 2 or 3 years when we restructured the entire frozen foods division and I had to run that whole operation alone. Don't you agree that I have the characteristics you want?"
Stress benefit	"And, from what you've told me, the primary thing you want to accomplish is to get your new Spiderweb silk operation going, is that correct? Since you're familiar with what I've accomplished in new product development, aren't you confident that I can do this job very well?" (Wait.) "You can relax, knowing you have a seasoned professional handling this department."
Close	"Would you please tell me if you are ready to make a decision now, or would you like to set up an appointment for a second meeting?"

Another objection you're likely to hear is: *I need to think it over!*

You: *"I'm so pleased that you're interested enough in my working here that you'd like to think more about it. May I ask what in particular you would like to consider further?"*

By asking that question, you're reducing a vague, general notion, which you cannot really deal with, to something specific, which you can handle.

> OR

You: *"Is there anything you would like to ask? I hope I've covered everything, but if I haven't, wouldn't it be better to discuss that now so you'll have the information you need?"*

Some Closes That Will Help You Get an Offer[5]

While all of these closes are professional, it is not the techniques but the way they are used that conveys professionalism. Remember the smile and gentle manner. Be very sensitive to the impact you're having on the interviewer. If you begin to feel that your approach has been a little too assertive, you can always back off and say: "I'm so interested in this opportunity that I may have pressed a little too hard. If so, I'm very sorry."

Review of Three Closes

You have already learned at least 3 closes:

1. Choice close
2. Assumptive close
3. Similar situation close

1. Choice Close. As you know, this close offers a choice between something and something, rather than between something and nothing. That's what you did when you asked for an appointment. Which would you prefer: Monday or Tuesday? Nine a.m. or 9:30? Should we get together for lunch, or is breakfast more convenient for you?

Offering choices is a win-win formula. You give the other person some discretion, which makes him feel good. And you retain control, because both options are acceptable to you. By focusing on a smaller, simpler decision, like where—or when—to meet, you bypass the bigger decision: to meet or not to meet. You're making it easier for them to decide.

Similarly, instead of asking for the big decision—whether or not they want you for the job—you inquire which starting date is better for them. "When would you like me to start, on the first of the month or the tenth? In one week or two?"

If you're not convinced that the choice close works, try it with your friends or your children. "Would you rather have your story time before your bath or after? Would you like to clean your room before lunch or after?" Or ask your friend: "Should I drive or would you rather take your car? Would you rather have eel casserole or squid soup?" You'll be amazed by how much more cooperative people are when you offer choices.

2. Assumptive Close. It's your firm belief that they will want to hire you (or meet you). You've used this when you made your appointment with the hiring authority.

3. Similar Situation Close. This is also known as the Feel/Felt/Found close because of the language you use in your response. It is one way to overcome the objection that you do not have exactly the right experience. Initially, you're agreeing with the objection the decision maker raised. "Yes, I understand how you feel. My former employer felt that way until he found that I could learn their industry so quickly that I was generating new business within 2 months."

Additional Closes

1. Tie-down Close. You probably use this all the time, without knowing that it has a name. It's wonderful because it's so natural. And easy! The tie-down is simply asking for an agreement.

"That's really easy, isn't it?"

"You agree with me, don't you?"

"That's a terrific idea, don't you think?"

You can tie down at the end of the sentence or begin with it.

"Don't you agree that this will be really beneficial?"

"Isn't it a good idea to have everyone here?"

Once you get in the "tie-down habit," you'll find that it's easy to get continuing confirmation from people you're talking with, including hiring authorities. One agreement leads to another. Since your conversation has been so harmonious, it should be easy to ask: Don't you agree that I should be part of your team?

2. Trial Close. This is a test question that you ask in order to get the decision maker's preliminary opinion.

"Is that what you had in mind?"

"Isn't that the kind of person you want in your department?"

3. Puppy Dog Close. While Johnny begged his parents to buy the puppy, the pet store owner listened to the parents' misgivings. They were concerned that Johnny was too young to take proper care of the puppy.

"Try it for a week," the proprietor suggested. "Give Johnny a chance to show how well he'll do. And if it doesn't work out, you can return Spot at no charge." Once the puppy was home, of course, no one could imagine returning the adorable, cuddly pet.

"Try it. You'll like it." Employers love temps because they can try out employees without making long-term commitments. Temps dramatically reduce the risk and make it easy for employers to buy. Despite certain obvious disadvantages, temporary employment also provides a chance to try different kinds of work in a variety of settings.

As an entrepreneur, you are your own temp service and you really need to close when you are face-to-face with the decision maker. The puppy dog close makes it easy for you because you're offering to:

- provide a specific service on a contractual basis.
- work on a trial basis.

AFTER THE CLOSE

What Do You Do after You Have Asked a Closing Question?

Nothing! Keep quiet! Silence is your biggest friend. Don't underestimate how difficult it is to keep quiet. Practice it with a friend. Ask a closing question. Then time the silence. You'll be amazed by how endless a minute of silence seems. Bite your tongue, if necessary. But don't say a word after you ask a closing question. The ball's in their court.

Eventually, he'll do something:

1. He will offer you a job.
2. He won't make you an offer and will explain his reason(s). That gives you a chance to overcome that objection and close again.
3. He'll remain noncommittal—and you can try another close.

Essential Elements

In your meeting with a decision maker, you must:

- Get his attention
- Build interest through benefits you could bring
- Create desire
- Get a commitment

To summarize the art of closing:

1. Ask for the offer.
2. Make it easy for them by asking for a small decision.
3. Sum up professionally.
4. Get something started, possibly on a trial (puppy dog) basis.

Closing is the last step in the process of persuasive communications, which includes assessing yourself, setting your goal, planning and preparing, asking the right person, listening actively, presenting a good case, emphasizing benefits, overcoming objections, and closing. Having closed—asked for a decision—does not mean you're finished. You'll be putting these same skills to very good use as you follow up and negotiate your compensation for your job.

EMPLOYMENT INSURANCE CHECKLIST

✓ Are you aware that a close is just a request for a decision?

✓ Why are your emotions high when you ask for a job?

✓ Why are their emotions high when you ask for a job?

✓ Why do some employers insist that you ask for the job?

✓ Why is it that each time you meet a decision maker, you can increase his interest in you?

✓ And as soon as you leave, his interest wanes?

✓ What you do after you close?

✓ Are you getting agreements throughout your meeting?

✓ Do you make it easy for them to buy your services by asking for small decisions and offering either a choice or a puppy dog or both?

CHAPTER 16

❖

It Ain't Over 'til It's Over: Following Up

Should I follow up?

How?

When?

Which is better? A letter or a phone call?

If it's a letter, what should it say?

How often should I call back?

How can I be sure I'm not being a pest?

It looked like the job was mine. How can I find out what went wrong?

HOW CAN YOU INSURE A HAPPY ENDING?

Questions about following up are almost as numerous as those about how to get the appointment in the first place. And they're just as important. You'll probably be asking them even though you've done everything right, because few people get jobs at their first meeting. It usually takes more contacts—follow-up calls and letters, plus two or three meetings—to get an offer.

Don't Drop the Ball

Job seekers often make very good impressions initially. Then they drop the ball. Whether the culprit is lack of confidence, poor organizational skills, or sheer laziness, the result is the same. Someone else picks up the ball and runs with it.

Develop an Effective Strategy

Use an active three-pronged approach:

1. Continuing persuasion
2. Evaluating this opportunity
3. Active job hunting with other potential employers

Prong one is continuing persuasion. You're keeping in touch with this employer, directly and indirectly, using a combination of patience and persistence for as long as it takes. That could be weeks, even months. All this time, you're still trying to impress them in any way you can, to clarify any misunderstandings that may have developed, and to add new, relevant information.

Prong two is ongoing information-gathering and assessment about the company, the opportunity, and the people you would be working with. You're evaluating them so you can decide whether or not to accept their offer when it comes.

The third prong is active job searching. Pinning all your hopes on one possible job is dangerous. Despite your excellent qualifications and follow-up, it might not work out. If you've been focused on only this possibility, you're apt to get awfully discouraged. Getting geared up to start again from the bottom of the mountain is terribly difficult. So, your best insurance is to keep lots of balls in the air—keep contacting and meeting decision makers while you're actively following up.

IMMEDIATE FOLLOW-UP

Post-Meeting Self-Evaluation

Immediately after your meeting with the decision maker, analyze it. Review it thoroughly while the experience is still fresh in your mind. The notes you took at the meeting are probably very sketchy, so now's the time to fill in the blanks. (Another option is to tape your thoughts about the meeting.) You could do that right in your car, if that's convenient, or as soon as you get back to your desk.

Take a piece of paper and answer the questions on the Interview Debriefing Form on page 201. They'll help you organize your ideas so you can do an even better job next time.

INTERVIEW DEBRIEFING FORM

Company name   Date

Address   Telephone

Meeting with

Title

Others

Name(s)

Position title

Hiring authority

Did I ask good questions?

Did I analyze the hiring authority's needs?

Did I focus my presentation on those needs?

Did I emphasize how I would benefit them?

Did I present evidence (mini-stories)?

Did I speak and act like an equal?

Did I anticipate and answer objections?

Was I interested and enthusiastic?

Did I get little agreements?

Did I ask for the job?

Did I ask for a summary?

Did I schedule a second meeting?

What did I do really well?

What could I have done better?

What is my follow-up plan?

Other comments

Thank-You Letter

Whatever the outcome of your meeting, a brief thank-you note to the hiring authority is a *must*. Check the spelling and titles of everyone you write to. Mistakes here could be disastrous. Who could blame the prospective employer for thinking: If he misspells my name before he's hired, what will he mess up later?

This kind of warning should not be necessary, but misspelled and misdirected thank-you letters from applicants, including college graduates, are all too frequent.

Should it be handwritten or typed? Handwritten notes may appear warmer, more personal, and more memorable. That's a plus. But most job seekers prefer typing their letters. Once you have a core letter on your computer, you can personalize it appropriately for individual recipients.

When should you send it? It should be in the mail within 24 hours. If the employer has requested something which is not immediately available, write the thank-you note, explaining that the requested material will be forwarded ASAP. Then, follow through on that.

What should it say? Basically, your letter includes three messages:[1]

1. Thank them for their time and consideration
2. Emphasize your interest in the job:

    ◆ your desire for it
    ◆ your confidence that you can do it
    ◆ the benefits you would bring

3. Retain the initiative for further contact, stating that you are looking forward to meeting them again.

- ♦ If a meeting has been set, refer to that specific date.
- ♦ If a meeting has not been set, write that you will call at a specific time. Then do it! If you have written that you will call
next Tuesday, make a note in your tickler file for Tuesday.
And call.

Optional: Relevant information not covered in your meeting could be
included here.

The decision maker's colleagues should also receive your thank-you
letters. Since few applicants even think of writing to various other people
they met during their visit, this little courtesy is a chance to set yourself
apart. Thanking people cannot hurt and could even be decisive in a close
contest.

YOUR NEXT STEP

Your Strategy

Recalling the Level of Interest/Time chart in Chapter 15, you want them
to keep you in mind, positively, of course. Your strategy is to:

1. Keep your name before them.
2. Rekindle their interest.

Who Else Can Help You?

Having others speak on your behalf is, of course, much more potent
than doing it yourself. Now's the time for your strongest references to
call or send letters to the hiring authority and/or others who might have
input into the decision. For example, influential people in other organizations or board members might carry a lot of weight with the decision
maker.

Be sure they understand your point of view and how much you can help
the organization, as well as how much this opportunity means to you.
Depending on the kind of position you're looking for, lobbying by others
could be decisive. This is not, of course, the kind of thing you can do
without having a strong network, especially good relationships with business friends.

What You Can Do Yourself

Think of ways to add information that might be helpful and/or interesting, either by phone or mail.

Phoning. The timing and frequency of your calls depend on several factors, including their time frame. Hopefully, before your meeting ended, you got some sense from them regarding follow-up and determined a convenient time to phone.

Unless there is some good reason not to, call back within a week from the time they will have received your thank-you letter. You might say:

"I'm calling to see if there's any additional information you'd like to have."

OR

"I'm calling to see if I can be helpful to you in any way."

OR

"I'm calling to ask about your plans for a second meeting. Would you like to schedule one now, or should I call back later this week?"

This may be a bolder approach than you're accustomed to using. But think of it this way. You sincerely believe that you'll be an asset to the organization. And they need you. You're just trying to get them off the fence so both of you can benefit.

Mailing or faxing. Watch for articles that are relevant to their business, a mutual interest, or something they might appreciate. Have you received an invitation or meeting notice they might be interested in? You could send a copy and write that you hope to see them there. Or even offer to give them a ride. Keep demonstrating that you are alert to what's going on and showing interest in them. That communication is persuasive. And that's what following up is all about.

Persistence, Not Annoyance

Are you concerned about "overdoing it"? Afraid you'll ruin your chances if you're too persistent? Your anxiety is understandable. This is a balancing act. And there are no fixed rules. But job seekers tend to be overly cautious—still hoping for the white knight to do the job.

Often, they don't call back after the interview. Or they call back once, find out no decision has been made, and drop the ball. You certainly don't want to be obnoxious. But I've never heard of anyone losing out on a job because they wanted it *too* much. On the other hand, I know of many people who *got the job because they wanted it so much.*

It Ain't Over 'til It's Over

One example. A nonprofit organization was recruiting a marketing director. Mr. Abel, the executive director, had interviewed several qualified applicants and selected one.

Before he offered the position to "Ms. Best," Janet called, explained that she had just heard about this job, and asked for an appointment.

"Sorry," replied Abel. "We have already interviewed several very qualified people and we've selected the best person. The job is filled."

Most people would have given up right there. Not Janet.

"Have you made her an offer yet?" she asked.

"No, not yet."

"Please don't make any offers until you see me. You'll be glad you waited. I can come to your office this afternoon or tomorrow morning, if that's better for you."

You know the rest. Janet got the job. Her spirit and determination were just what the organization needed. It was a happy ending for everyone. Except, of course, for "Ms. Best."

MULTIPLE INTERVIEWS

Now You Have an Ally

Once you've passed the screen test, you know that at least one person thinks you're right for the job. Identifying your advocate should not be too difficult when you return for your second meeting. If it's the hiring authority, you're in luck. But in this case, it's John, a staff member you'd be working with. You and John hit it off right away and you're both sure you'd work well together.

John can be very helpful in convincing the hiring authority, who is on the fence. You might ask John what they regard as your strengths—and weaknesses. Or any reason(s) they're hesitating to hire you. Then you know what objections you have to overcome.

Meeting More Future Colleagues

You could have several more individual, as well as group, meetings. People who have different kinds of responsibilities in the organization tend to have different perspectives. The president, for example, may just want to "check you out," briefly, but might also be interested in you as a person. You might expect a broader perspective from that individual than the person you're reporting to. But there are no guarantees.

In general, your best strategy is to do what you've done so well already. Be positive, confident, and friendly. Listen. Focus on them and their needs. Be reassuring, show how well you'll fit in, and emphasize how you can benefit them. Eventually, you'll reduce their anxiety about making a decision and they'll make you an offer.

IF YOU DON'T GET THE JOB

Murphy's Law

"The interview really went well. It looked like the job was mine. But now, they're not returning my phone calls."

OR

"They decided against hiring anyone after all."

It's not unusual. You thought everything was fine. Then you reach an impasse. Why? The hiring process is very complex. Their decision not to hire you might have nothing to do with you. It could be that their need (or their perception of it) changed. Maybe a Janet (or a nephew) appeared from nowhere.

How Do You Look at It?

Rejection is part of the job search process. No matter how good you are, it's going to happen. But it's not the setbacks that count as much as the way you handle them. When you read the biographies of notables in virtually every kind of endeavor, from Abraham Lincoln to Art Buchwald, it's amazing how many hardships and difficulties they had to overcome. "Success," said Winston Churchill, "is going from failure to failure without losing enthusiasm." Life gives all of us lemons. Here are some suggestions for making something out of it.

Recipe for Lemonade

1. Mix in some self-assessment. If you can learn something from the experience, that helps. Review your Interview Debriefing Form to see if you can pinpoint where things may have gone wrong. What could you do differently or better next time?

2. Mix in their input. You can ask why you didn't get the job. Getting some honest feedback would be great, wouldn't it? After you've cooled down, you might decide to approach the hiring authority this way:

"Ms. Simpson. I've received your letter. I'm really disappointed that you've chosen someone else. I was so excited about the job and I know I would have done it well. Since I'm still looking for a job, it would really help me a lot if you would tell me what I might have done better or differently."

But how does this make Ms. Simpson feel? Uncomfortable. Maybe a little guilty. The person she chose may really be better qualified. Or maybe she was simply more pleasant. What can Ms. Simpson say? Even if she really wants to help, she has to worry about the legal consequences of anything she says. So she avoids mentioning age, gender, disability, race, weight, appearance, personality, accent, etc.—any one of which could have been the real reason for her choice.

You might luck out and get some useful suggestions. But more likely, you'll hear that you interviewed very well but that the other person simply had more experience.

3. Make a friend. Another approach is to salvage the situation by encouraging an ongoing relationship. That could work well if you have something in common with the decision maker.

"Ms. Simpson. I'm so disappointed, I can't tell you. I was really excited about this job, and I was looking forward to working with you. I can appreciate that you need someone with a stronger background in systems analysis right now. But since we seem to have so much in common, I thought we could stay in touch. How about getting together for lunch either Wednesday or Thursday?"

That's better, isn't it? You've spared Ms. Simpson a guilt trip and begun a new relationship. She's now a part of your network and could even become a business friend. And, if the "more experienced" person doesn't work out, what a perfect position you're in![2]

Ms. Simpson was, in fact, so relieved by the applicant's positive response that she gladly met for lunch. Before long, she heard about a similar position and happily recommended her new friend.

4. Obtain referrals. Another response to being turned down is to write a nice letter or call, thanking them for considering you and asking for the names of 2 or 3 non-competitors who might benefit from meeting someone with your credentials.

5. Maintain contact. No matter how disappointed you are, keep a positive relationship with them—and stay in touch. They might need you in the future.

THE FRUITS OF FOLLOW-UP

Persistence Pays

Eventually, your patience and persistence will pay off. You've persuaded them. They want you!

When You Get an Offer

- ◆ You may want to accept it, if it's what you want, and if you have enough information to negotiate effectively at this time. (See Chapter 17 on Negotiations.)
- ◆ **Don't reject it.** Thank them for the offer, continue to show interest, and ask for some time to think about this important decision. You may be able to transform an initially poor offer into something worthwhile. Ask them how soon they would like to have your response. Be definite about when you will answer. And keep your promise.

EMPLOYMENT INSURANCE CHECKLIST

- ✓ Did you do an evaluation of your meeting?
- ✓ What did you do well?
- ✓ What can you do better next time?
- ✓ Did you write thank-you letters?
- ✓ Are you keeping in touch with them?
- ✓ What are you doing to rekindle their interest?
- ✓ Is your job search still very active?
- ✓ Are you asking your referrals to help you?
- ✓ If you didn't get that job, did you make lemonade?
- ✓ What did you learn from this experience?
- ✓ Did you vow to do a better job next time?

C H A P T E R 1 7

Negotiating Your Compensation

SETTING THE STAGE

You've done everything right. After three meetings with the CEO and other top people at Chocolate Cowpies, the thriving gourmet catering company, you're feeling great. They like you. And you're eager to get to work as their new vice president for product development.

"How Much Will It Take to Bring You on Board?"

That's the music you've been hoping to hear. You're ready to dance and you *assume* they're prepared to hire you. But their question could mean something else, for example:

> This guy looks terrific. But we probably can't afford him. We'd better find out how much he wants so we don't waste more time if he's out of our league.

So when you say: "Well, I thought $100,000 plus company car and membership in the club, etc., would be a good place to start," you've confirmed their worst fears. You'd never be happy with the $80,000 they had in mind. So they wrap up the discussion. And the music stops.

> Or maybe they're thinking: Her credentials are excellent and we think she could do a good job for us. We'd better find out what she's willing to work for.

When you say "$45,000," they're amazed. That's about $10,000 less than they were prepared to offer. *Now* they're thinking: Maybe she's not as good as she looks. We'd better think about this a little more. We want to be sure we get the right person for this job.

You're already familiar with *Salary Rule #1: Do NOT discuss compensation until you have a firm job offer.* It's repeated here because foot-in-the-mouth disease is, unfortunately, so common. There's NO advantage to you in giving them a salary figure. There are only disadvantages.

Why, then, do so many people blurt these things out? It's a sign of inexperience—but it's not limited to younger people. Obviously, it's because they're not thinking about the consequences of what they're saying. When people ask, we're apt to respond truthfully and tell them what they want to know.

A Better Response

Honesty is indeed the best policy, but remember your objective. You want several job offers so you can make the best choice. If you're being pressed for your salary requirements but still don't have a firm offer, why not ask for it? Simply say: "You have asked me several times how much I expect to earn. I'm curious. Does that mean you're offering me the job?"

If they say "yes," congratulations! Now you have something to work with. If their answer is something else, you're back to square one: persuading them to make you an offer.

Salary Rule #2: Wait for Their Salary Offer

After they offer you the job, express your appreciation and interest, but keep holding off on the salary question until they give you a figure. Just toss the ball back to them by asking:

"What salary did you have in mind?"

OR

"I'm sure you have a salary range for people in this kind of position (or for people with my credentials), don't you?"

Employers are sometimes remarkably vague about salaries, but they are decision makers. When they offer you a job, they have some idea of what they'd be willing to pay. Usually, they have quite a specific salary range in mind. Keep asking, politely, pleasantly, and persistently. That's how you play the game.

Example. After Erik, a young chemist, was told that they wanted him for a research position at IBM, the human resources manager asked Erik what salary he wanted. Erik just continued to smile and ask, "What's your salary range for a new Ph.D.?" The ball bounced back and forth several times. Finally, the HR manager offered $53,000. Silence really is golden, Erik thought, as he quickly calculated the difference between their figure and what he would have asked for: $35,000. Keeping quiet had just earned him $18,000 a year!

If the range they give you seems satisfactory, you could say something like:

"The upper part of that range would be acceptable."

OR

"Don't you agree that the higher figure is appropriate, considering how much I bring to this job?" You are, of course, prepared to justify the higher figure.

THE GAME OF NEGOTIATIONS

You Already Know How to Play

Just as finding this job meant learning about yourself, the company and the job, and persuasive communications, to negotiate effectively you'll need information about yourself, this employer, and the negotiating game. The good news is that now you have a head start. Obviously, you're persuasive. You've convinced this employer to meet you and offer you a job. Negotiating is a specialized form of persuasive communications. In both cases, you're convincing others to do what you would like them to do.

The word *negotiations* sounds intimidating, evoking images of silver-haired diplomats in pin-striped suits, conferring around a massive table in an elegant salon. But negotiating, like persuading, isn't foreign at all. It's something we all do every day—working out little common-sense agreements that make our lives livable. It's deciding how you're going to spend your day off with your friend, or which movie to see on Saturday, or figuring out what your family wants for breakfast.

Negotiating Consciously Is Advantageous

You've negotiated all your life, probably without thinking about it too much. By consciously playing this game and adjusting your behavior accordingly, you'll not only get better compensation for this job, but you'll improve your results in other situations as well.

Once again, knowledge is power. The more you know in advance about yourself, them, and the process, the better.

PREPARATION: KNOW YOURSELF

Your Needs

You're back at the beginning: self-knowledge. Start by analyzing your own situation, especially your financial and emotional condition.

1. Your financial situation. Ask yourself:

What do I *want?*

What do I *need?*

Businesspeople use assets/liabilities balance sheets to get a financial overview of how things stand. By preparing your own balance sheet, you can get that valuable perspective and calculate what you need: your bottom line.

Take a piece of paper and list your financial obligations on the liabilities side. Then list your assets on the other side. Look at your total monthly expenses and determine what you need to earn.[1] It's good to know what your basic, immediate needs are, but don't limit yourself to these costs.

Consider your age and assets also. Even though you may be in your thirties, it's not too early to begin thinking about how much you'll need to retire and how much you'll have to save now to achieve that sum. Don't forget that the salary you negotiate now is the basis for all your future financial arrangements with this company. Regardless of how hard you work and how much you accomplish, any raise you get—usually a percentage increase—will be based on your starting salary. Today, you're their number one candidate: don't sell yourself short.

On the other hand, if you've had a good income and have accumulated substantial resources, like Ben, the 60-year-old lawyer, you may not need such a high income at this time. Only you can determine what you really need.

ASSETS/LIABILITIES BALANCE SHEET

Assets	*Liabilities*
savings bank	mortgage/rent
stocks	utilities
bonds	car payments
mutual funds	food
house	credit card debt
car	entertainment
	etc.

How much you *want*, of course, is another matter. You might want the moon, but will your credentials rocket you there? Assessing the contribution you will be able to make in this position and how quickly you can make it will help you determine your value to them right now. Will you be productive immediately—or will it take 6 months of training before you can have much of an impact? How directly is this job related to the company's profits?

2. Your emotional and other needs. Money, of course, is not your only need. Your emotional needs may be more pressing. If you're terribly unhappy in your current job or are unemployed and feel it's urgent that you get something, you're not, of course, in a strong negotiating position.

Your attitude and self-confidence are critically important here. How much do you value yourself and what you have to offer? You may be a gem—brilliant, talented, and blessed with extraordinary abilities. But if you don't think you're worth much, they won't either. It's like the dusty old painting in the attic that was discarded because the owners thought it was worthless. It took someone else to recognize its value and appreciate his rare find. Unless you have a benefactor, you have to be the one to recognize your own value.

How would you feel if you didn't reach an agreement? To a large extent, your strength or "relative negotiating power" depends on "how attractive . . . is the option of not reaching an agreement."[2] How urgently do you need this job? Are all your hopes pinned on this offer? Or do you feel that you can find (or have found) something equally good—or better?

The standard advice is: Don't quit one job until you have another. You'll not only feel more in control; you'll look better to employers. It's a cliche that when you're employed, you're more employable. In fact, many recruiters will not even consider you unless you *are* employed.

But that may not be an option for you right now. If you're unemployed, the best way to gain a sense of control and negotiating power is to get several job offers. That's why using the *Employment "Insurance"* approach is so valuable.

Your Specific Objective and Overall Goal

Just as you need a goal to guide your job search, you must decide *what* you want to get out of these negotiations *before* you start. Are you clear about the difference between what you *want* and what you *need?* How much of a gap is there between what you want and what you'll accept (your bottom line)?

As you gather information, make a list of what you want and prioritize it. What's really important to you? And what can you be flexible about? If your title and the size of your office are not that meaningful to you, make a note of that. You might want to make another list of questions to ask so that everything is as clear as possible before you make a commitment.

You can help achieve a win-win agreement—where you get the compensation you want and they're satisfied that the agreement is fair. By being empathetic and flexible, you can help make that happen. You're communicating that you're part of their team, searching for a mutually satisfactory agreement: "I know you'll want to pay me what I'm worth."[3] Because you're prepared, you're confident and calm. Your achievements and the benefits you will bring strengthen your case.

Focus on what's important to you and be flexible about the rest. For example, they want you to start in one week but you would prefer to remain at your present job for a month or two, although there's no compelling reason to do so. You could resolve the difference in favor of your current employer. That means giving them at least two weeks' notice and doing everything possible to minimize the disruption your departure will cause.

Your new employer will understand when you explain why you cannot start in less than two weeks, emphasizing your responsibility to your employer. That's quite different from saying it would be more convenient for you to start in a month or two, apparently disregarding their urgent need.

PREPARATION: KNOW THEM

Compensation Information about Them and the Marketplace

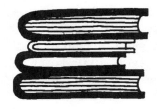

What do you know about compensation for comparable work in this organization? Their competitors? For a national perspective, ask your librarian for the *American Almanac of Jobs and Salaries*,[4] *Occupational Outlook Handbook*,[5] and *American Salaries and Wages Survey*.[6] In addition, many professional and other organizations do salary surveys of their memberships and publish the results in appropriate journals. Information about librarians' salaries, for example, is published in the *Library Journal*.

These national figures will give you a solid base of information, but regional and local cost-of-living differences should also be taken into account. Talk with knowledgeable people, including recruiters and people in the industry, to get up-to-date information about this kind of job. Ask about salary ranges, benefits, and special incentives, like sign-on bonuses. Whatever you can learn about this particular company—salaries and what kinds of benefits are negotiable—will give you a big advantage.

If you've been offered an unusual position, getting reliable information might require some sleuthing. Bill, a young dentist, had just created a unique position for himself as the head of a proposed dental services unit for a health plan. A practicing dentist, Bill had spent an entire year developing his proposal and getting the requisite approvals.

Now they were ready to dance. But because this position was just being developed, there was no job description. And no title. Bill didn't know what to call this job, what compensation to expect, and how to respond to their forthcoming offer.

The significance of his title went way beyond ego. Bill's status and reporting relationships in the organization, as well as his compensation, depended on whether he was a director or a manager. He felt strongly that the level of his position was crucial to the success of his proposed unit. Happily, the information Bill needed was available, indirectly, from some recruiters of medical executives and he was able to negotiate the entire package successfully.

Objective facts are invaluable. They can be your star witnesses as you make your case for a good compensation package.

Their Needs

Hiring authorities have needs too. Even in a buyers' market, their negotiating power, like yours, depends on how attractive the option of not reaching an agreement is.[7] How urgently do they have to fill this particular position? And how well do you fit in? Hiring decisions reflect the decision maker's personal needs, as well as those of the organization. Do you know exactly why you were selected for this job? Was it your expertise? Your connections? Because the boss likes you?

It could be timing. And the fact that you asked for the job. Ron, a new systems engineering manager, had been interviewing people for months, and the many candidates he had seen were starting to blur in his mind. His boss was fretting about the time Ron was spending and worried that he was incapable of making a decision. Ron's colleagues were anxious because they needed the new hire to help meet an upcoming deadline with their most important customer. By the time you interviewed, almost everyone was questioning Ron's managerial ability.

You were qualified. Not more qualified than the others, to be sure. But you were there when Ron felt he had to choose. By asking when he would like you to start—next Monday or the first of the month—you made his decision easy! Now he had what he urgently needed: proof that he was decisive. And you had your offer. By presenting clear options, you helped him make that tough decision and showed him how valuable you are.

In general, the company's negotiating position depends on the availability of people with your particular skills in the marketplace. Are they in short supply? Knowing about the company's time frame, how well you fit in, and the availability of people with comparable skills will help you negotiate.

WHAT CAN BE NEGOTIATED?

Everything

Salary is the key piece, of course, but there are many others. Too many job seekers assume that the organization's offer is set in stone. And they have only 2 options: take it or leave it. By recognizing that everything—benefits, working conditions, as well as salary—may be negotiable, you increase the chances of reaching a good agreement. That does not mean that everything in every situation is negotiable, but that there's probably more leeway than you have realized.

Benefits

Benefits are the fastest-growing component of compensation, accounting for more than 40% of the total. While some perks, like country club membership and executive parking, are declining, others, like child-care facilities, are increasing. Among the benefits that may be negotiable are:

health
profit sharing
pension/retirement (company match on 401K plan)
life insurance
company car/car allowance
tuition aid
sign-on cash bonus
performance or other bonuses
home office equipment
flextime
extra vacation
severance

If you are relocating, consider relocation expenses, including temporary housing, placement services for your spouse, etc.

Performance/Salary Review

One way to improve your salary is to negotiate the timing of your first performance review. For example, you could have a review and *upgrade* in 2 months, instead of 3, 6, or more months.

Bonus/Profit Sharing

Salary plus arrangements could be mutually beneficial. The timing and percentage of bonuses and/or profit sharing are subject to negotiation.

Other Aspects of Your Job

Will you have the staff, equipment, and support necessary to fulfill your responsibilities? Now's the time to ask for what you need so you can do the best possible job for them—and yourself.

Richard was very pleased when he accepted his position as a counselor for a not-for-profit organization. Initially, there were three grants supporting the work he loved to do—helping clients find jobs. But within a year, the funding ran out and Richard was urged to market the agency for his own, and their, survival.

Although some of the proposals he wrote were funded, the agency would pay him only for his billable hours, the hours he spent in direct service to clients. He was in the frustrating position of having to volunteer his time to get the funds to do his job for which he would be paid. Richard found himself, inadvertently, self-employed.

Additional Responsibilities

In general, you'll want to be as indispensable as possible to your new employer and to develop yourself as fully as you can. Most people wouldn't want to take on added responsibilities at the outset, but there might be good reasons to do that. For example:

1. Although this is a good company and you want this job, it's too similar to what you've done and you want more challenge.
2. It doesn't pay enough. If you could get enough support (personnel, equipment, or whatever is necessary), you would be willing to combine elements of more than one job. By doing that, you can help them streamline and save money. If additional training is required, training time and cost should be factored into this agreement.
3. You think there's more growth in a related activity, and you want to get one foot in that door.

Working Arrangements

Flextime and doing some work from home are some additional things to consider. These kinds of arrangements could make a huge difference in how well this job works out for them, as well as for you.

THE BALL'S IN YOUR COURT

The Importance of Listening

"Listen to them with respect, show them courtesy, express your appreciation for their time and effort, emphasize your concern with meeting their basic needs. . . ."[8] Listening is as crucial for successful negotiations as for persuasive communications. Follow the 70%:30% rule—listening 70% of the time, speaking only 30%, mostly asking questions. There's no advantage to revealing a lot about yourself right now. Keeping your ears open, on the other hand, will allow you to pick up details you might otherwise miss. Example:

Them:	"We just can't pay you more than $50,000 right now."
You:	"By "right now," what do you mean?"
Them:	"We're hoping to have a couple of big contracts under our belt by the end of the year. Then, we'll be in a stronger position."
You:	"I see. Are you saying that if these contracts come through in the next 3 months, you might be able to pay me $55,000, assuming I do an excellent job, of course?"
Them:	"Well, maybe."
You:	"Then why don't we schedule our performance/salary upgrade review for December 30, rather than March 30?"

Your Strategy

As in the past, you're "them" oriented. Keep emphasizing how you can benefit them as you work towards narrowing the gap between what they offer and what you want.

The discussion will probably start with the most important item: salary. Benefits will follow. If the salary is not as high as you had hoped, you can try to compensate with a better benefits package.

How hard should you push? That's a delicate balance and again, there are no "right" answers. You'll want to negotiate a good deal for yourself—and the best time to do it is now, when they want you. But obviously, squeezing out their last dollar is hardly the way to embark on a good long-term relationship.

On the other hand, job seekers often don't get what they're entitled to, either because they never thought to ask—or were afraid they'd seem too pushy. That's why your research is so important. Everyone respects facts. And skilled negotiators.

What Are Your Options?

Essentially, you have three:

1. Accept their offer
2. Reject their offer
3. Ask for something else

1. If their offer is very good and you feel ready to make a commitment, accept it.[9] But there are some advantages to asking for a little time before you make the commitment:

- ◆ It's usually wise to discuss the offer with someone you trust
- ◆ You may think of questions, issues which should be clarified before accepting. Are you sure you're not making some unwarranted assumptions?

  Note: If you request some time to consider their offer, be sure you agree on a deadline. When would you like a decision: Thursday or Friday? Then, meet that deadline.

- ◆ There may be another offer(s) to consider. You may be able to use this offer to leverage another. Example: You call the hiring authority in company B and explain that you have received an offer. You would prefer to work with B, but must give company A an answer before (deadline). Can B meet or exceed A's offer? It's worth a try. People tend to want what they can't have. Your offer from another employer (which remains nameless) makes you more desirable.

2. Even if you're quite sure you will refuse the offer, *don't reject it on the spot.*[10] Express your appreciation for their offer and keep the door open for possible future contact.

If you do reject an offer, be empathetic. Compliment them, if you can do so sincerely, to soften the rejection. Example: "This is such an interesting company and working with you would be a terrific challenge. But I know what my financial responsibilities are and I just cannot accept your offer. Why don't we stay in touch so that if things change, maybe we can work something out?"

They may be able to make you a better offer at a later time. Or they may refer you to another non-competing organization. In any case, try to salvage the situation by becoming business friends.

3. Ask for something else. What counteroffer can you make? The number of possible scenarios is vast. We'll focus on two and suggest some responses you could make.

a) Their offer is acceptable. It meets your needs and the gap between you is not too great.

Example: They offer $40,000. You were hoping for $45,000.

One option: Show how small the $5,000 gap is by reducing it to the ridiculous.[11] When you spread the $5,000 over a period of time, it almost disappears. For example, "Did you realize that $5,000 over a year is only $13.70 a day? That doesn't seem like too much to invest in a top-quality person who will undoubtedly generate more than that within the year, does it?"

OR

Review the list of benefits to see where you might be able to make the difference. You might, for example, focus on their bonus. "I'm sure I can make enough of a difference in the first two months that you'll agree that I'm worth that bonus."

Another option: Split the difference. You might prefer to forgo the $2,500 because: "I really think this would be a good chance for us to work together. Why don't we just split the difference?"

b) The offer is poor. It would meet your barest needs, but would significantly change your lifestyle.

Example: They offer $45,000. You were earning $75,000. The gap seems to be too wide to bridge.

Huge disparities between previous earnings and current offers are not so unusual. Employers are, understandably, trying to get the best for the least. And job seekers sometimes feel insulted by this "bargain hunting." As time passes, they often lament: "I turned down some offers months ago. They were so low I didn't think I could accept them. But now, I have nothing."

It's the classic "half a loaf" dilemma. Again, no simple "right" answer. That depends on how you perceive your situation, as well as objective conditions. If their offer is much lower than you feel you can accept, you might consider some alternative arrangements with them:

◆ Part time, rather than full-time

◆ Consulting for a specific project

◆ Consulting for a specified period of time

You are suggesting these alternatives because you feel you cannot accept the low salary for a full-time job.

> *"I can understand that you can't pay me what I'm worth on a full-time basis. But you know that my _____ experience is what you need right now, and I would like to help you get to the next stage of your strategic plan. Maybe we can work something out on a more limited basis so you can get past this hurdle."*

Note: The focus is on helping them—not on keeping the wolf from the door.

If you can work out something on an interim basis, there are several advantages to you:

1. You are working, which usually translates into improved self-esteem.
2. You are earning some income.
3. Depending on the nature of your duties, you're in contact with other potential employers through your work.
4. The situation may change and more resources become available.
5. You see other possibilities once you're inside the organization, perhaps leading to a full-time position.
6. You can keep looking for more and better opportunities.

Too Many Job Offers?

What a great problem to have! *Three* good opportunities. Now you have to choose which is best for you. Writing down your thoughts in the form of the Ben Franklin (or balance sheet) close can help you do that. Take a sheet of paper and make a list of the major factors affecting your decision at the three companies. Assign a value from 1 to 10 to each of these factors, with 10 having the highest value.[12]

Comparisons of Job Opportunities			
Factor	*Company A*	*Company B*	*Company C*
Title			
Salary			
Benefits			
Major duties			
Location			
Advancement opportunity			
Corporate culture			
Caliber of management			
Reputation			

When you've assessed each job this way, you should be able to reach your decision more easily.

Confirmation Letter

A handshake is usually enough. Once you have agreed on the terms and the starting date, you've got a deal. But it's always a good idea to get your offer in writing, especially if you will be quitting your job or moving to another location. Most organizations would be happy to write a letter, but if they were not planning to do so, you could make it easy for them. Use the same technique you used to get reference letters. Draft a letter, including the major points of your agreement: salary, benefits, major responsibilities, starting date, etc. After they have sent it to you, you can respond with a brief letter of acceptance.

You Did It!

By conducting yourself well during your negotiations, you're starting your new job on a high note. They might even see your negotiating ability as a big plus. Now that you're on their team, you can negotiate for them. If you can do that with a sense of humor, that's even better.

Now it's really time to celebrate. You have your new job! You've planned, prepared, practiced, and pursued opportunities until you found a really good one. Best wishes in your new position! Isn't it great to know that by following these methods, you can insure your employment future!

EMPLOYMENT INSURANCE CHECKLIST

✓ Do you know yourself, your needs and wants, your immediate objective and long-range goal?

✓ Do you know them, what they need and want?

✓ Do you know what's negotiable?

✓ Do you have a positive, win-win approach?

✓ Are you negotiating like a professional, being empathetic, and being a good listener?

✓ Do you know that by planning, preparing, practicing, and persistently following through, you'll get more than a job? You'll have employment security!

N O T E S

❖

Chapter 1

1. "Work and Family: Jobs Held and Weeks Worked by Young Adults," data from the National Longitudinal Surveys, Report 827, U.S. Department of Labor, Bureau of Labor Statistics, August, 1992, p. 1. "By age 29, a typical young worker has held 7.6 jobs and worked 434 weeks since age 18." The report also refers to an earlier study. "One estimate claims that two-thirds of the total number of job changes occur in the first 10 years of an individual's career." Based on that estimate, it seems safe to conclude that the average young American worker will have to find at least ten jobs in his/her working career.

2. Louis Uchitelle's article, "The Rise of the Losing Class," *New York Times*, Nov. 20, 1994, Section 4, pp. 1, 5, provides an excellent analysis of how "a changing economy is gradually linking highly educated managers and technicians with high-school-trained assembly-line workers and office clerks. . . . What they share, public opinions polls show, are feelings of uncertainty, insecurity and anxiety about their jobs and incomes."

3. Charles Handy, *The Age of Unreason* (Cambridge, MA: Harvard Business School Press, 1989), p. 31. Handy's analysis of organizations and the workforce is reiterated in his more recent book, *The Age of Paradox* (Cambridge, MA: Harvard Business School Press, 1994).

4. Tamar Lewin, "Low Pay and Closed Doors Greet Young in Job Market," *New York Times*, March 10, 1994, pp. A1, A12.

5. Handy, p. 64.

6. *Inc. Yourself: How to Profit by Setting Up Your Own Organization* by Judith H. McGuown (New York: Macmillan Publishing Co. 1977), is a book about incorporating your business. The excellent title is borrowed here because it communicates so effectively what job seekers should do to transform how they think about themselves—from employees to independent, self-employed persons.

7. Although 351 is not a large sample for survey research, the results are meaningful because they reinforce our experience with thousands of job seekers. See the Appendix for the questionnaire.

8. Technology now allows employers and job applicants in different parts of the country to "meet" and conduct initial interviews via video phones. For example, Management Recruiters International, Inc., the largest contingency search firm in the world, offers long-distance interviewing via AT&T video phones. Typically, however, employers will not make a final hiring decision prior to a face-to-face interview.

9. Jerry Hill, Vice President of Training, Management Recruiters International, Inc., was the major instructor for Sale to

Success. His definition of selling is telling the truth attractively.

Chapter 2

1. Jeannemarie Caris-McManus, CEO, Western Reserve Collaborative, a management consulting firm.

2. Herbert A. Shepard, "On the Realization of Human Potential: A Path with a Heart" in Michael B. Arthur, Lotte Barilyn, Daniel J. Levinson, Herbert A. Shepard, eds., *Working with Careers*. (Columbia University School of Business, 1984), pp. 179, 175.

3. Meetings with Dr. Donald K. Freedheim and Dr. Dianne Tice, Department of Psychology, Case Western Reserve University, Cleveland, Ohio, March 25, 1993 and July 9, 1993, respectively.

4. The material in "Some Exercises for Probing Deeply" is from Professor Donald M. Wolfe's course: Self-assessment and Career Development, Weatherhead School of Management, Case Western Reserve University, Cleveland, Fall, 1993.

Chapter 3

1. Rick Hampson quoting Ben Feldman in "World's Greatest Insurance Salesman," *Plain Dealer* (Cleveland), Nov. 28, 1993, pp. 1E, 5E.

2. The *Dictionary of Occupational Titles* (DOT), a publication of the U.S. Government, published by the Superintendent of Documents, U.S. Government Printing Office, Washington, DC 20402, was most recently updated in 1991. While it contains much useful information, a 1991 publication is obviously limited.

3. U.S. Government Printing Office, address above.

4. These techniques were described by Jerry Hill.

5. Belleruth Naparstek, *Staying Well with Guided Imagery* (New York: Warner Books, 1994), p. 51.

6. Ibid. Psychotherapist Naparstek explains: "This entails imagining yourself already in the condition or circumstances that you wish for. . . . you don't need a lot of technical information to do this kind of imagery correctly. You just have to know what you want."

7. The following exercises were developed by Jerry Hill:

RELAX. Forget everyone around you. Close your eyes. Take a few deep breaths. Don't force them. Let your breath out slowly. Take a deep breath. Let it out.

Imagine yourself six months from today. You have achieved your goal. Keep your eyes closed. Where are you? What does it look like? Picture where you are. What does it smell like? Sweet? Sour? Musty? What is it like outside? Cold? Warm? Listen for the sounds around you. What kinds of noises do you hear?

How did you attain your goal? What are other people saying to you? Are they proud of you? What are they saying about you? Six months from today, where are you located? What does it look like? Smell like? Is it cold? Warm? How do you feel? What does it feel like now that you have achieved your goal? When you have that picture—that whole scene—firmly in your mind, you can open your eyes.

Chapter 4

1. Letters from Scott Simon and Ray Suarez, Sept. 27, 1994.

2. Meeting with Mary Ellen Crowley Huesken, February 3, 1993.

3. Rosabeth Moss Kanter, *When Giants Learn to Dance* (New York: Simon & Schuster, 1989), p. 321.

Chapter 5

1. Jeannemarie Caris-McManus.

2. Jerry Hill.

3. Robert E. Maher, President, American Management Development, Inc., an executive outplacement company headquartered in Cleveland.

4. Jerry Hill and Louis R. Scott, VP, Corporate Development (Ret.), Manage-

ment Recruiters International. Scott's interviewing workshop for Sale to Success participants was one of the most valuable elements of the program.

5. Louis R. Scott.
6. Scott and Hill.
7. Scott and Hill.
8. Louis R. Scott.

Chapter 6

1. Louis R. Scott.
2. Jeannemarie Caris-McManus.
3. Jerry Hill.
4. Jerry Hill.
5. Jerry Hill.
6. Jerry Hill.
7. Jerry Hill.
8. Edwin C. Bliss, *Doing It Now* (New York: Charles Scribner's Sons, 1983), p. 124.

Chapter 7

1. The term "business friend" originates with Carol E. Rivchun, marketing consultant, Cleveland. She defines a business friend as someone you get to know after 4 or 5 meetings, who shares some mutual interests, and with whom you develop a mutually beneficial relationship.

2. *Encyclopedia of Associations*, 29th ed., Carol A. Schwartz and Rebecca L. Turner, eds. (Detroit: Gale Research, Inc., 1995).

Chapter 8

1. Richard Nelson Bolles, *The 1995 What Color Is Your Parachute?* (Berkeley, CA: Ten Speed Press, 1993), pp. 28–29.
2. Louis R. Scott.
3. Louis R. Scott.
4. Louis R. Scott proposed this rule.
5. Joyce Lain Kennedy and Thomas J. Morrow, *Electronic Job Search Revolution* (New York: John Wiley & Sons, 1994).

Chapter 9

1. Louis R. Scott.

Chapter 11

1. Jerry Hill.
2. Jerry Hill.

Chapter 12

1. Jack Gubkin, "Persuasive Communications: The ABCs of Selling" (unpublished manual), p. 13. Gubkin's outline of the approach, which describes the selling process, has been adapted here as a job search tool. Gubkin was the instructor for the first three Sale to Success courses in 1983.

2. Jack Gubkin, course in Persuasive Communications sponsored by Greater Cleveland Growth Association's Council of Smaller Enterprises, 1981.
3. Gubkin, p. 54.
4. Ibid., p. 55.
5. Ibid.
6. Gubkin, p. 57.
7. Jerry Hill.

Chapter 13

1. Jerry Hill and Louis R. Scott described this method and provided most of the responses to objections used in this chapter.
2. Jerry Hill and Louis R. Scott.
3. Jerry Hill and Louis R. Scott.

Chapter 14

1. Jerry Hill.
2. Louis R. Scott.
3. Louis R. Scott.
4. Louis R. Scott.
5. Louis R. Scott.
6. Louis R. Scott.
7. Louis R. Scott.

Chapter 15

1. Louis R. Scott's favorite way to sum up a meeting with a hiring authority.
2. All three Sale to Success instructors, Jack Gubkin, Jerry Hill, and Louis R. Scott, emphasized the necessity of closing.
3. Louis R. Scott.

4. Jerry Hill has used this level-of-interest/time diagram to explain the need for closing early and often.

5. Jack Gubkin.

Chapter 16

1. Louis R. Scott.
2. Carol E. Rivchun.

Chapter 17

1. Doing an assets/liabilities balance sheet prior to your meeting with hiring authorities was recommended by Louis R. Scott.

2. Roger Fisher and William Ury, *Getting to Yes* (New York: Penguin Books, 1981), p. 106.

3. Louis R. Scott.

4. John W. Wright, *American Almanac of Jobs and Salaries, 1994-5* (New York: Avon Books, 1992).

5. *Occupational Outlook Handbook*, 1994-95 edition, compiled by U.S. Department of Labor, Washington, DC.

6. Marlita A. Reddy, *American Salaries and Wages Survey—1993*, 2d ed. (Detroit: Gale Research, Inc.).

7. Fisher and Ury, p. 106.

8. Fisher and Ury, p. 56.

9. Louis R. Scott.

10. Louis R. Scott.

11. Jack Gubkin.

12. Louis R. Scott.

APPENDIX

Participants at an informal job seekers' seminar that was offered monthly by the Greater Cleveland Growth Association voluntarily completed this questionnaire. Three hundred and fifty-one participants completed the following survey during the period November 19, 1992, through January 20, 1994.

JOB SEEKERS' MARKETING SURVEY

Like many job seekers who participated in this survey, you may find that completing it is helpful. It enables you to begin an assessment of some of your marketing capabilities—your strengths and weaknesses. The survey is designed to help you help yourself by identifying which steps in the job-search process have become stumbling blocks and which skills you may want to work on.

Please check the most appropriate response. Double check if you strongly agree or disagree.

1. You keep hearing that you must have a positive attitude when looking for a job, but you find that very difficult to achieve most of the time.

   _____Yes; _____No; _____Other (please specify).

2. Most of the time, you are feeling:

   _____angry; _____fearful, panicky; _____hopeful;

   _____self-doubt, loss of self-esteem; _____loss of identity;

   _____depressed; _____confused; _____lonely; _____ashamed;

   _____confident; _____other.

3. From the above list, please TRIPLE CHECK the one word which best describes how you feel most of the time.

4. You have at least one trusted friend or spouse in whom you can confide all your hopes and fears.

   _____Yes; _____No; _____Other (please specify).

5. You have experienced major challenges before and coped well. You will do that again in this job search.

   _____Yes; _____No; _____Other (please specify).

6. Of all the challenges you have faced in your life, being unemployed is the most difficult.

   _____Yes; _____No; _____Other (please specify).

7. On the average, how many hours per week do you spend actually LOOKING for (NOT worrying about) employment?

   _____32-40 hrs.; _____20-31 hrs.; _____10-19 hrs.; _____0-9 hrs.

8. You have assessed your skills, talents, achievements, strengths, interests, etc., and know what marketable skills you can offer, what you are selling.

   _____Yes; _____No; _____Other (please specify).

9. You have set and WRITTEN your employment goal.

   _____Yes; _____No; _____Other (please specify).

10. You have assessed your basic needs (financial and other) with your spouse/partner and can survive financially for at least 6 months.

    _____Yes; _____No; _____Other (please specify).

11. You have developed a marketing plan which identifies your target market and how to reach it.

    _____Yes; _____No; _____Other (please specify).

12. You have researched your target industry/organizations through printed, online, and other resources.

    _____Yes; _____No; _____Other (please specify).

13. To obtain information and explore possible opportunities, you network daily (on the average) with:

    _____10 or more people; _____4-9 people; _____1-3 people; _____no one.

14. You know that meeting with and persuading a hiring authority (a decision maker with the authority to employ you) is the crucial part of the job-finding process.

_____Yes; _____No; _____Other (please specify).

15. On the average, you meet with _____ (number of) hiring authorities each month.

16. You believe you can be persuasive with hiring authorities once you meet them, but you have not been able to set up enough appointments.

_____Yes; _____No; _____Other (please specify).

17. Are you allowing your fear of hearing "no" delay your employment by months (or years)?

_____Yes; _____No; _____Other (please specify).

18. You are a good investigator, asking many open-ended questions to learn about the decision maker and the organization—their needs and possible opportunities.

_____Yes; _____No; _____Other (please specify).

19. You are a good listener, able to concentrate actively on what the other person is saying.

_____Yes; _____No; _____Other (please specify).

20. You know how to overcome objections, such as "You're overqualified" or "You have no experience in our industry."

_____Yes; _____No; _____Other (please specify).

21. You know how to ask for—and get—a decision.

_____Yes; _____No; _____Other (please specify).

22. You always follow up meetings with hiring authorities (and others) with thank-you notes and continue to follow up until (and after) a decision has been made.

_____Yes; _____No; _____Other (please specify).

23. You have been unemployed:

_____up to 3 months; _____4-7 months; _____8-12 months; _____13-18 months; _____19 months or more.

24. Your unemployment is due to INVOLUNTARY separation (including "early retirement," etc.).

_____Yes; _____No; _____Other (please specify).

25. Your previous annual earned income level was:

_____$30,000 or under; _____$31-45,000; _____$46-60,000; _____$61-75,000; _____$76,000 and over.

26. You expect your future earnings to be:

_____much higher; _____higher; _____about the same; _____lower; _____much lower.

27. Your gender:

_____male; _____female.

28. Your age:

_____under 35; _____36-49; _____50-62; _____63 and over.

29. The most difficult aspect of being unemployed is:

_____

30. You understand that all the skills you need to find employment can be learned, often in a few hours.

_____Yes; _____No; _____Other (please specify).

31. You would like to be self-employed eventually, if not in the immediate future.

_____Yes; _____No; _____Other (please specify).

INDEX

ABOUT THE AUTHOR

A career management consultant and president of Step to Success, Annette L. Segall has helped thousands of people find jobs, change careers, and become self-employed. Many of these people benefited from innovative programs that she created, including Sale to Success, TeleConnect, and SaleSense. More than 82% of Sale to Success' 1,100 graduates found employment within 90 days of program completion.

Job-finding, career management, and coping with employment anxiety are among the subjects she addresses in articles for the *National Business Employment Weekly* and other major publications. A Ph.D. in political science, she has taught graduate and undergraduate courses and also addresses corporations, professional and business organizations.

NOTES

NOTES

Order Form

To order *Beyond Blue Suits and Resumes*,
please complete all information below and send to:

Step to Success
P.O. Box 18432
Cleveland, Ohio 44118-0432

Please send _____ copies @ $14.95

Shipping and handling per copy   3.95

Sales tax (Ohio residents add 7%)   _____

TOTAL (U.S. funds only)   _____

For information and quantity discounts, please call 216-932-9638.

❑ CHECK   ❑ MONEY ORDER for $_____ payable to **Step to Success**. For MasterCard or Visa orders, please call 800-263-STEP.

Account # _____ Expiration _____

Signature _____

Your Name _____

Address _____

City/State/Zip _____

Daytime phone _____

THANK YOU VERY MUCH FOR YOUR ORDER
YOU MUST BE SATISFIED OR YOUR MONEY BACK

What People Are Saying about
Beyond Blue Suits and Resumes

"This is an excellent book! I wish the people I've interviewed over the years had read this book and gotten themselves prepared. Anyone reading this gets the hands-on, how-to information they really need."

Theodore Rudolph, CLU, ChFC
Agency Vice President
CIGNA Financial Advisors

"I know these principles work. They instill vital self-confidence. Whether you're employed or unemployed, read this book—and read it again!"

Lloyd D. Mazur
Attorney at Law and
Vice President of Real Estate
Dalad Group

"This book is a GIFT to anyone seeking employment. Read it! Use it! You will get the job!"

Walter J. Hoag, Assistant Director
Ohio Department of Insurance

"Practical and comprehensive. This book is an up-to-the-minute guide to enhance employability in the current market. A must-read for those who are willing to take responsibility for their work life."

Susan R. Hurwitz, M.A., L.P.C.

"Amazingly well written. It will be a great help to anyone who uses it."

Richard Boyatzis, Ph.D., Professor
Weatherhead School of Management
Case Western Reserve University